INVITATION
TO ARCHAEOLOGY

James Deetz is Professor of Anthropology at the University of California at Santa Barbara, where he also directed the Field School in Archaeology during the summers of 1961, 1962, and 1964. He received his B.A., M.A., and Ph.D. from Harvard University, where he spent 1965–66 as a visiting Associate Professor. He has published many articles on North American archaeology and ethnography and has served as Archaeological Adviser to Plimoth Plantation in Plymouth, Massachusetts, since 1961.

American Museum Science Books are published for The
American Museum of Natural History by The Natural
History Press. Directed by a joint editorial board made
up of members of the staff of the Museum and Doubleday, this series is an extension of the Museum's scientific
and educational activities, making available to the student and general reader inexpensive, up-to-date, and reliable books in the life and earth sciences, including
anthropology and astronomy. The Natural History Press
is a division of Doubleday & Company, Inc., and has its
editorial offices at The American Museum of Natural
History, Central Park West at 79th Street, New York,
New York 10024, and its business offices at 501 Franklin
Avenue, Garden City, New York.

INVITATION TO ARCHAEOLOGY

James Deetz

WITH ILLUSTRATIONS BY
ERIC G. ENGSTROM

AMERICAN MUSEUM SCIENCE BOOKS

Published for The American Museum of Natural History
THE NATURAL HISTORY PRESS
Garden City, New York
1967

Invitation to Archaeology was published also
in a hardbound edition by The Natural History Press.

American Museum Science Books edition: 1967

CONTENTS

PREFACE

"Archaeologists dig up Indian bones and study old things to make money." This is an eight-year-old boy's answer to the question: "What do archaeologists do, and why?" Yet it is not too different from answers given to the same question by a large portion of the lay public. On the other hand, an eleven-year-old boy answers with: "They study early man, his habits, weapons, and goods, to find out what we originated from." This particular eleven-year-old happens to be my son, and may not be a fair example; but the definition and explanation actually came from a sixth grade unit in social studies, and not from me. These two responses, and the differences between them, make an important point. The field of archaeology is coming into public awareness more and more, but it is an imperfect awareness. Although elementary education is providing understandings which produce answers like the one above, the average person does not really know exactly what archaeology is all about or why anyone would consider making it his life's work. This book is an attempt to present in brief form the essential hows, wheres and whys of archaeology. It is not a textbook treatment of the subject but a consideration of the many complexities of archaeology through example rather than exhaustive description.

Perhaps a word or two of explanation are in order with regard to some of the specific examples and illustrations chosen. They reflect the author's particular viewpoint and background, and as such are rather heavily biased in the direction of material which is historical and even non-archaeological in the orthodox sense. While no apologies are offered for this particular choice, it is perhaps useful to explain that it reflects in part a point of view which is not necessarily shared by all members of the archaeological profession. It is hoped that much of what is different here will eventually become a part of the "mainstream" of archaeological method, but at this writing such is not necessarily the case, and the reader should know this. In those few cases where true conjecture enters the picture, an effort has been made to make it quite clear that it is just that; otherwise, although the manner of presentation may be a little different, most of the material represents archaeology as most of us know it. In some ways, this book is really more a statement of how an archaeologist thinks, or at least how one individual does, than it is a summary of what he thinks about. A detailed outline of the results of archaeological research would be out of place in a book of this kind; there are several excellent summaries of this type some of which are given in the Bibliography.

Whether part of what is written here is somewhat unorthodox in terms of conventional archaeology is not as important as the fact that this book has been written in the hope that it can in one way or another make clear the approach of modern archaeology. At a time when it is not unusual to see a group of people digging carefully into the earth along the highway, when national news magazines regularly carry articles about exciting and significant archaeological discoveries, and when archaeologists make news of sufficient importance to be included in the first section of the newspaper, archaeology can no longer be thought of as the rather relaxed pastime of bearded scholars wearing pith helmets and searching for lost treasures or, for that matter, only for Indian bones.

Chapter I

WHAT IS ARCHAEOLOGY?

Archaeology is the special concern of a certain type of anthropologist.[1] We cannot define archaeology except in reference to anthropology, the discipline of which it is a part. Anthropology is the study of man in the broadest sense, including his physical, cultural, and psychological aspects, and their interrelationships.[2] Archaeology concerns itself with man in the past; it has been called the anthropology of extinct peoples.

Archaeologists are anthropologists who usually excavate the material remains of past cultures, and through the study of such evidence, attempt to re-create the history of man from his earliest past and to determine the nature of cultural systems at different times and places around the world. Archaeology is similar to history in part of its purpose, that of delineating sequences of events in the past and their importance to mankind today. This kind of reconstruction is called prehistory, a term which stresses a basic difference between archaeology and history. Prehistory treats the time before man learned to write and therefore record his own career on earth. It begins with man's first appearance on this planet, almost two million years ago, and usually ends with

[1] This book is concerned with archaeology as a part of anthropology. There is a somewhat different type of archaeology, sometimes called classical archaeology, which is primarily concerned with the archaeology of the civilizations of the ancient Mediterranean world. This type of archaeology is usually taught as art history in university art departments. Its beginnings lie in the Renaissance, when man became interested anew in ancient art and dug it from the ground to serve as an example and inspiration. Anthropological archaeology, on the other hand, is only as old as anthropology itself, and is concerned with all the remains of past man, wherever we find them in the world.

[2] Excellent general introductions to anthropology include D. L. Oliver, *Invitation to Anthropology* (New York: Natural History Press, 1964) and F. Keesing, *Cultural Anthropology* (New York: Holt, Rinehart & Winston, 1958).

the beginnings of written history in all parts of the world. This later date can be as early as *circa* 3500 B.C. in the Near East, or as late as A.D. 1850 in parts of the state of California. While such time limits can be imposed on archaeological studies, they are somewhat flexible and blurred at the later end of the scale. In recent years, archaeologists and historians have become aware of the value of working together in certain situations. The archaeological and historical records combined often yield a richer picture than either would separately. We know from history that Plymouth Colony was founded in 1620, that the ship bringing the first colonists was the *Mayflower*, that separate land grants were given the settlers in the cattle division of 1627, and that the first houses were probably made from sawn clapboards. Yet no known historical documentation tells us exactly what animals were used for food by the Plymouth colonists, what types of dishes were used in the homes, when the first bricks were produced locally, or what types of nails, window cames or door hardware were used in constructing the houses. Archaeological investigation of seventeenth-century house sites in Plymouth has given the answers to all these questions, fleshing out much of the bare bones of the historical accounts.

In the missions of southern California, we know from the historical record that quarters were constructed for the Indian neophytes, and that they were occupied by family groups. Such a structure was built at La Purisima Mission in 1814, but the resident Padre was satisfied with simply noting in his diary that the building had been erected. Archaeological excavation showed it to be 540 feet long, of adobe brick with heavy tile roof. Study of the contents of the apartment units within this barracks structure provided valuable insights regarding Indian life in the missions not forthcoming from the historical record.

If historical documentation is of value at the later end of the archaeologist's time scale, the earliest end leans heavily on the natural sciences. The older the material, the less perfectly preserved it usually is, and the greater the need for supporting interpretations with data drawn from other disciplines. The excavation of a 40,000-year-old site in France requires the assistance of paleontologists, botanists, soil specialists, and geologists, to name but a few of the non-anthropological scholars who work with the archaeologist in the analysis of the materials recovered. Through the application of results from these supplementary fields, the archaeologist is given a good idea of the environment in which man lived at the time, and the types of problems which life presented.

The "where" of archaeological work is as important as the "when." Modern archaeologists are pursuing their investigations in all those places where man lives or has lived at any time in the past. Sites are excavated in the frigid Arctic, in the jungles of tropical America, Africa and Asia, on the open plains of the United States, beneath the streets of London, and even under the waters along the coastlines of many parts of the world.

With the entire world from which to draw his materials, and a two million year span of time represented by them, it is the task of the archaeologist today to integrate this immense yet imperfect corpus of data into a meaningful picture, and in so doing provide an understanding of cultural process in time and space.

Culture

Archaeology seeks to learn about culture from the fragmentary remains of the products of human activity. What, then, is culture? Culture can mean many things: a growth of bacteria in a petri dish, the correct way to behave in various situations, or what we get when we read "good" books, listen to "good" music, or learn to appreciate "good" works of art. To the anthropologist, culture means none of these things. On the other hand, to say just what it does mean to an anthropologist is by no means simple. In fact one entire book has been devoted to the definitions of culture used in anthropology.[3] Assuming that you could find them, ten anthropologists selected at random on the street would probably give ten somewhat different definitions.

[3] A. L. Kroeber, and C. Kluckhohn, *Culture: A Critical Review of Concepts and Definitions* (Papers of the Peabody Museum of American Archeology and Ethnology, Vol. 47, No. 1); Cambridge, 1952.

Since we are concerned with culture in our discussion of archaeology, we must attempt a definition in the face of so many others; there is some comfort in numbers, however, and our treatment of culture in this case will not be too different from the consensus. Culture can be defined by making several statements about it.

CULTURE IS LEARNED BEHAVIOR. We inherit many things from our ancestors through genes; the color of our hair, our blood type, the shape of our face. Other things are given to us by our ancestors, but not biologically. There is no gene for speaking English, wearing a necktie, calling our mother's sister's children "cousin" or using Arabic numerals. Yet, generation after generation does these things, having learned them by a process separate from the genetic and biological, a process termed *extrasomatic*, apart from the body. We might even say that culture is everything a person would not do were he to grow up completely isolated on a desert island.

CULTURE IS UNIQUELY HUMAN. This statement might cause some disagreement. Many species of animals learn certain patterns of behavior in a way not too different from that by which man learns cultural patterns. But man is the only animal who uses culture as his primary means of coping with his environment. Culture is man's adaptive system. While bears and rabbits in the Arctic have developed heavy pelts through biological evolution that protect them against the cold, the Eskimo makes a snug fur suit and lives in an igloo. Over the ages, man has elaborated culture into an ever more complex buffer between him and his world. Remove this cultural screen from the picture, and we would find man so ill adapted to his environment that he would probably become extinct. Even a brief loss of electrical power places urban man in an unfamiliar and uncomfortable relationship to the environment, and an apartment dweller who cannot use his electric can opener is in much the same predicament as an Australian aborigine who has lost all his spears while hunting far from home.

CULTURE IS PATTERNED. The array of habits and customs which make up culture for any group of people is integrated: each part relates to every other part in a systematic manner. Anthropologists categorize culture in certain conventional ways. Language, religion, economics, technology, social organization, art and political structure are typical categories. In any culture, the form of the political structure is in some way contingent on the social structure; art reflects religion, social organization shapes a part of technology, and so on. In studying the nature of cultural patterning, anthropologists have come to understand how culture is structured in hundreds of cases.

SOCIETY IS THE VEHICLE FOR CULTURE. The distinction between culture and society is clear. Societies are groups of interacting organisms, and man is but one species of social animal along with other primates, many insects, and even certain lower forms of life. In the human case, society is the repository of culture; it carries it; its members participate in it; and culture is the dominant determinant of social behavior.

Culture can thus be defined as a uniquely human system of habits and customs acquired by man through an extrasomatic process, carried by his society, and used as his primary means of adapting to his environment.[4]

To this definition we might add one qualification as archaeologists. Culture is highly perishable, and therefore cannot be excavated. No one has ever dug up a political system, a language, a set of religious beliefs, or a people's attitude toward their ancestors. Yet such things as political and religious behavior, language, and social interaction affect what the archaeologist does recover. The patterning which the archaeologist perceives in his material is a reflection of the patterning of the culture which produced it. Pots, arrowheads, house floors and axes are the products of culture, not culture in themselves, but they are linked to culture in a systematic manner. It is the archaeologist's task to discover how cultural behavior is shown in its products.

[4] Anthropologists also distinguish between culture on the one hand, and individual cultures on the other. This latter, somewhat different use of the term signifies individual groups of people the members of which share in a particular culture system. Thus we can speak of American culture, Chinese culture, Navaho culture, etc. Another definition of culture in these terms would be the shared habits and customs of a single society.

Archaeological method

An Indian village on the Missouri River in 1750 must have been a lively place. Barking dogs running between large earth-covered houses; children playing on the roofs; women making pots and chatting by the doorways; a party of men returning from a hunting expedition laden with bison meat—all contribute to a picture of confusion, sound, and motion. The same village in 1965 is a silent cluster of dim green rings of grass on the brown prairie, the only sound that of the wind, the only motion and life that of a tumbleweed rolling across the low mounds and depressions, and of a hawk circling high in the sky. The people are gone, and the only things which attest to their former presence are fragments of the objects which they made and used, buried in the collapsed remains of their dwellings.

If you had gone into this village after all the people had left, but before any deterioration had begun, understanding what had taken place there would be difficult enough. The material culture of a people is but a small part of their whole cultural pattern. The behavior which took the form of chatting, playing, and hunting could not be directly observed in their absence. Add to the problem the factor of disintegration over a period of two centuries, and the magnitude of the archaeologist's task becomes painfully clear. He must attempt to say as much as he can about the entire way of life of a people based on the very fragmentary remains of only a fraction of their material products. It is this incompleteness of the archaeological record which demands many of the techniques and methods of archaeology.

Like physicists, chemists, biologists, and other scientists, archaeologists observe, describe, and attempt to explain. Observation, description, and explanation comprise the three levels of archaeological study, and the archaeologist proceeds through these levels in a certain way so that he might finally be able to say many things about past cultures based on their scanty and imperfect remains.[5] The particular operations of

[5] For a discussion of analytical levels in archaeology and anthropology, see G. R. Willey, and P. Phillips, *Method and Theory in*

archaeology which correspond to these somewhat general levels are the *collection* of data through excavation (observation), the *integration* of the data recovered by placing it in time and space and ordering it according to some type of classification which will permit comparison with similar data (description), and the drawing of *inferences* from the patterns seen in the integrated data which serve as explanations of these patterns in cultural terms (explanation).

At the first level, that of excavation, archaeologists have developed a set of field techniques which enable them to gain a maximum amount of useful information from the material buried beneath the earth. Having recovered this material in a carefully controlled way, it is necessary to bring order to it before any logical inferences can be made. At this second level of analysis, the primary goal is to describe the materials according to three variable dimensions, those of space, time, and form.[6] The spatial dimension of archaeological data is usually simply a function of the location of the excavations in terms of geographic space. To place the materials in time, a set of methods exists which enables the archaeologist to say how old his materials are. The formal dimension of archaeological materials consists of their physical appearance. Until the broken pots, remains of houses, flint arrowheads, and other fragments have been described in such a way that they can be compared with others, it is difficult to produce sophisticated inferences. The descriptive level of archaeology then consists of saying where the material was found, how old it is, and what it looks like—a seemingly simple set of operations which is in fact quite complex, and which has posed problems which have required almost philosophical solutions at times.

When he has recovered his evidence, and integrated it according to its spatial, temporal, and formal aspects, the archaeologist turns to the third level, that of asking what his materials mean in terms of the culture which produced them

American Archeology (Chicago: University of Chicago Press, Phoenix Books, 1962), p. 4.

[6] A. C. Spaulding, "The Dimensions of Archaeology," *Essays in the Science of Culture in Honor of Leslie A. White*, ed. G. E. Dole and R. L. Carneiro (New York: Thomas Crowell and Co., 1960).

in the distant past. At this level, four important aspects of the data become important for the first time; we can classify these aspects as the contextual, the functional, the structural, and the behavioral.

Let us see how these aspects are used in archaeological inference by considering how they relate to a specific case, a clay bowl for example. The contextual aspect of this bowl refers to the context in which it was found, and all the circumstances of its occurrence, including the animal and plant remains found with it. Inferences concerning the cultural meaning of this bowl would certainly differ if it had been discovered in a burial rather than in a house or on the altar of a ruined temple. In one case, it may have served a very special mortuary function; in the others, it may have been either a domestic object or a ritual one.

The contextual aspect of an object frequently tells us something about its functional aspect. However, it may not if the context of discovery was not identical to its functional context in the culture which used it. Bowls used for ritual, domestic, or mortuary purposes could all find their way into a common trash heap; we would certainly not suggest that this context indicated the use of this type of bowl as trash. The functional aspect of an object is at times clarified by the contextual aspect but may involve other considerations, since inferences regarding the function of the object in the culture which produced it involve the consideration of its contextual aspect as well as its functional aspect.

All man-made objects are reflections of the thoughts of the people who made them. The structural aspect of the bowl tells us something of the cultural norms which led to its production. In comparison with other bowls, this one might be seen as "typical" in that it and similar ones resulted from the expression in clay of a set of ideas which were joined by certain "rules" of combination. For example, since all bowls of this type have round bottoms and straight sides, there may have been a "rule" which dictated the repeated combination of round bottoms and straight sides, and bowls with square bottoms and flaring sides would violate such a "rule" and either would not have been made or would have been thought "wrong" by their makers.

The "rules" which govern the structural aspect of the bowl were a part of the cultural system of its makers, and as such were passed along from generation to generation. The repeated application of these "rules" shows a patterning of behavior which is reflected by the behavioral aspect of the bowl. That is, we are now concerned with the relation between the behavioral significance of patterning shown by the material and the behavior which was typical of the producing culture. For example, it has been shown that highly patterned and similar behavior led to the manufacture of similar pottery in an Indian village where women resided in the same dwelling with their daughters. The sharing of behavior patterns by these women, brought about by their common residence, was reflected in the sharing of "rules" as shown by the pottery.

These four aspects of archaeological data which form the basis of inference thus involve the circumstances of discovery of material objects as these might aid in understanding their function, the function served by the objects in the culture which produced them, the rules which dictated their creation, and the behavioral aspects of the sharing and passing on of these rules. At the inferential level, the archaeologist is at last providing the flesh for the bare bones of his data, and, if done with care and imagination, such a procedure makes possible the delineation and ultimate understanding of past cultures.

Excavation

In many ways, the archaeologist's fundamental unit of study is the *site*. In simplest terms, and perhaps in a rather profound sense, a site can be defined as that place where an archaeologist digs. A more specific definition would be a spatial concentration of material evidence of human activity. While sites are frequently the remains of communities, they need not be, and frequently represent activities other than those involved primarily with residence and domestic activity. Examples include cemeteries, frequently adjacent to communities, but at times separate; hunting sites, often called kill sites, where animals were slaughtered by driving a herd over a cliff; ceremonial precincts which were the focus of some type of ritual activity, Stonehenge being a good example; or quarries where stone was removed prior to its fabrication into finished tools.

Archaeologists speak of sites as having *components,* a component being the distinguishable evidence of a discrete occupation or use of that site by a group of people. A single component site would be one which was occupied only once, while a multicomponent site would be one which was occupied repeatedly by the same or different people. That the same people could produce two or more components can be understood through considering the effect of a temporary abandonment of the site of sufficient duration to permit the archaeologist to discern discrete evidence of each occupation. Both time and space can contribute to differences between cultures. It is possible that two neighboring communities differ less at one point in time than does one group of people from its direct ancestors a century removed.

When archaeological investigations are begun in an area where little work has been done in the past, the first step is to conduct a survey. This involves going over the area on foot, by auto, or horseback, inspecting aerial photographs if available, and recording all sites discovered through this process. Frequently, test excavations are made in conjunction with the survey to determine site depth or number of components. Such excavations are usually one or two small pits.

The sites are given numbers, and a form is made out which provides essential information regarding location, size, possible age, state of preservation, and other key facts. Many site-numbering systems are used; one of the most popular is that employed by the Smithsonian Institution, the University of California, and a number of other agencies. Typical site numbers assigned according to this system are 39 BF 2 and 4 SBa 520. An archaeologist familiar with the system knows immediately that the first is in South Dakota and the second in California, since the first number designates the state according to its position in an alphabetized list of states, with California being the fourth and South Dakota the thirty-ninth.[7] The letters designate counties, Buffalo and Santa

[7] Hawaii and Alaska, admitted to the Union since this numbering system was devised, are given numbers 49 and 50, thus preserving the other forty-eight number designations.

Barbara respectively. The final number refers to the site within the county according to survey lists. Thus, the first number designates the second site surveyed and recorded in Buffalo County, South Dakota, and the second the five hundred and twentieth site recorded in Santa Barbara County, California.

When the survey has been completed, certain sites are singled out for excavation. The reasons for such selection are many and varied, and range from the site's apparent importance based on size, depth, or other factors recorded on the survey form to the impending destruction of the site by road construction, dam building, or housing project development.

Having selected a site for excavation, the archaeologist establishes a camp in the site's vicinity, or, if he is lucky, houses his crew in a nearby town. In the United States, the majority of archaeological field work is done during the summer months, and crews are often made up of college students, although local help is frequently used to good advantage. The size of the crew is dictated by the size of the site, the magnitude of the work planned, and the operating budget.

The first step prior to excavation involves the drawing of a scale map of the site, or, in the case of very large sites, the particular area to be excavated and its immediate environs. A point is then located somewhere on or adjacent to the site, and designated the *datum* point. The datum point is marked permanently, either with a cement post, steel pipe, or by locating it on a natural feature such as a small rock outcropping which is not likely to be moved or lost over the years. The datum point is very important, since it is the reference point according to which all excavations are located. In this way, if further work should be done in the same area at some later time it will be possible to determine where previous excavations were carried out. A site not tied in with a datum point is floating in space, and once the dirt has been replaced it is impossible to tell where the excavations had been placed.

The first excavation is usually not on the site at all, but at a point well away from the area thought to contain cultural remains. This pit, often called a *control* pit, is dug in order to learn the nature of the soils and deposits in an undisturbed state. Such a pit is usually excavated to a depth of several feet. Its function is to show the archaeologist what the deposits on his site were like prior to man's disturbance of them. Disturbances observed on the site can then be interpreted in part with reference to the known, undisturbed cross section in the same area.

Having prepared the map, established the datum point, and ascertained the normal condition of the deposits on the site, the archaeologist is ready to begin excavation of the cultural materials. This procedure is a very complex one, and we can only consider excavation in its most general terms. Excellent manuals of field techniques providing specific and detailed information on excavation are available.[8]

In general, one of two approaches is employed, depending on the nature of the site. Both are aimed at maintaining a rigorous control on the location of all material recovered. In one case, there may be no visible evidence of structural remains such as walls, depressions marking the floors of houses, or mounds suggesting some type of building. In this case, one usually begins by laying out a grid on the site, and using the squares of the grid as a guide to the location of excavated materials. For example, if we were to begin excavation in a shell heap on the coast of California, there would be no visible evidence of structures, and past experience would suggest strongly that none would be encountered. Lacking such remains, a grid of five-foot squares would be laid out on the site, covering the area which was to be excavated. In this way we are imposing an arbitrary order on an unstructured (to our eyes, at least) area of material. Our imposed, arbitrary order, in the form of grid squares, then serves as a guide to the segregation of specimens according to horizontal location. The squares are usually given co-ordinate numbers of one type or another. The usual procedure is to select an arbitrary point, which may also be the datum point, at the intersection of two lines, and give each square a number-letter code based on the cardinal points of the compass and distance from the

[8] R. Heizer, A Manual of Archaeological Field Methods (rev. ed.; Palo Alto: National Press, 1950).

K. Kenyon, Beginning in Archaeology (rev. ed.; New York: Praeger, 1961).

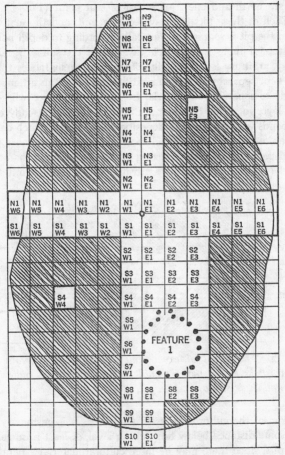

Fig. 1 *A small site (shaded area) showing layout of grid control. House circle (Feature 1) is excavated as a unit. Numbered squares have been excavated.*

point of departure. Thus a square just northeast of the point of departure would be designated N 1 E 1, since it is one square north and one square east of that point (Fig. 1).

Each of these pits is excavated as a unit, and the material from the pit is segregated vertically according to depth below surface. If there is no visible layering of the soil (stratification), arbitrary levels, usually either three or six inches thick, are kept separate. If visible stratification exists, an attempt is made to separate the material from a given pit according to the layer in which it is found. Such stratification usually corresponds with the discrete deposition of materials which could be quite different from level to level. If arbitrary levels are used there is a danger of mixing material from more than one level (Fig. 2). The pits are excavated in this manner until the

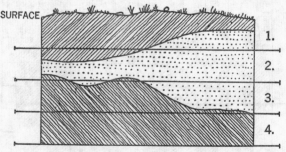

Fig. 2   The effect of excavating sloping natural strata by arbitrary levels. Level 2 would contain the mixed materials from all three strata.

bottom of the cultural deposits is reached. It is customary to dig some distance below this bottom level, at least in some of the pits, since there may be more cultural material separated from that above by a band of sterile, seemingly undisturbed fill.

The material recovered during excavation is placed in strong paper or cloth bags. Each bag is labeled according to the pit and level which produced the materials. A typical bag might carry the label:

4 SBa 7
N3 W5
0.5 ft – 1.0 ft B.S.
7/16/62
J.W.

The objects in the bag are known to have come from the second level below surface (vertical location within a half foot) in the third square to the north and the fifth square to the west of the key point of the grid (horizontal location within five feet) in the seventh site recorded in Santa Barbara County, California. Such a label provides a precise location of the contents of the bag. The date of excavation is given in the fourth line, and the initials in the fifth line are those of the digger so that, should any question arise concerning the material, the archaeologist will know who to consult (or in some cases, who to blame!).

A slight difference in labeling occurs if there are visible layers. In this case, these layers are numbered, and the vertical location is given according to layer number. Each digger working on a pit also completes a daily report describing the work he did, unusual circumstances noted, and any other information of importance. These notes are filed together and consulted frequently by the archaeologist as work progresses, and in the preparation of the final report of the excavation of the site.

When the presence of architectural features in a site is known, these frequently replace the grid as the main guide to horizontal location. In this case, there is an order inherent in the material, which the archaeologist can see. It is more logical to let this order dictate the location of materials whenever possible. For example, the site might be a multi-room pueblo in the Southwest. The rooms then become the basic units of horizontal location, since a completely random application of a grid could lead to mixing, much as the application of arbitrary vertical levels could produce mixing in the presence of visible stratification. If a square happened to cover parts of two rooms, and if these rooms served quite different functions, or were built and used at different times, unwanted mixing would be certain to result. Grids can be used with success within structural units, however, and often are useful when the structures are large.

Vertical segregation in structures is usually according to visible levels; at least an attempt is made to segregate material from the floor of the structure from the fill, that portion which was introduced at some later time, or through the collapse of a roof (Fig. 3). The difference between material

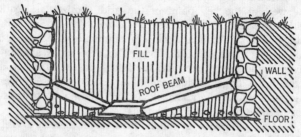

Fig. 3   Typical controls used in a collapsed room unit.

from the floor and fill of a structure is illustrated by a common case encountered in excavating the foundations of earth-covered houses in the Great Plains. In this case, the dirt used by the builders in covering the roof to a thickness of two feet was often removed from areas of the village which contained debris from earlier times. In many instances, this material was hundreds of years older than the house being built. When the village was abandoned, and the house either burned or collapsed, older material was deposited atop the later material on the floor of the house. Failure to segregate specimens according to whether they came from the floor or fill overlying the floor results in mixing materials which were made centuries apart.

A bag label from a site with structures might look something like this:

4 SBa 520
structure 22
room 6
floor

Those areas of sites with architectural features which lack such structures are excavated according to a grid system.

In the course of digging, the archaeologist encounters a variety of materials, which can be classified into three broad, general classes: artifacts, features, and non-artifactual materials. When associated, these constitute what is usually termed an archaeological assemblage. Artifacts are man-made objects such as pots, axes, pipes, arrowheads, or beads. Features are culturally produced objects which, unlike artifacts, cannot be taken from the field. They include fire pits, houses, storage pits, and burials, to name but a very few. The artifacts from features can be collected, but the features themselves must be recorded in the field. This is done by making accurate plans, cross-sectional drawings, and photographs of the feature. This information is filed with the other data from the site. Non-artifactual materials include a great variety of things, such as animal bone, seeds, charcoal, shells, pigments, asphaltum, and ash. While not man-made, such material tells the archaeologist much about the former occupants of the site.

When the excavations have been completed, and all records, artifacts, and related materials have been taken into the laboratory, the archaeologist is ready to begin the difficult but often fascinating task of resurrecting a life way of a people from the scraps and pieces which he has spent long hours removing from the earth. Before this can begin, the material must be cleaned and catalogued. Cataloguing is a simple process and involves placing a number on each object taken from the site. These numbers are entered in a catalogue, and the entry tells the location and circumstances of discovery of each object. Once a collection has been catalogued, it can be mixed, sorted, or segregated in any way, and it is still possible to place the objects back in their original relationships with an accuracy which is as great as the accuracy and precision of field location by pit, level, or feature.

Chapter II

DATING METHODS

The question "When?" is usually one of the first to be asked by the archaeologist. Since man has been littering the landscape for nearly two million years, the problem of assigning dates of reasonable accuracy to various samples of his litter is a complex one.

It is customary to distinguish two types of archaeological dating—relative and absolute. Relative dating is really not dating at all in the usual sense, but the placement of an assemblage in time relative to other assemblages. In assigning a relative date to assemblage B, we simply say that it is either older or younger than assemblage A, or that it occurred in time between assemblages A and C. Such relative arrangements ultimately tell us about a sequence of events—occupations of sites, developments in technology, hunting techniques, or architecture—but give us no idea about when this sequence took place in the past. To anchor a relative sequence in the continuum of time, absolute dates are needed. Absolute dates are given in terms of years ago, or years old; A.D. 1066, 35,000 B.C., A.D. 1963, and 1,750,000 B.C. are all absolute dates. By combining relative and absolute dates, we can describe sequences of events, and say when they took place.

Methods for obtaining relative dates are quite different from those used in absolute dating. Two commonly used methods of relative dating are *stratigraphy* and *seriation*. While a number of other methods are also used, these two will serve as good examples of some of the basic principles involved.

Stratigraphy

Stratigraphy proceeds on the basis of interpreting the layering of archaeological deposits. Multicomponent sites are built up over the years by the constant deposit of debris atop debris. Logically, the deeper in the site a layer is, the older it is. This layer-cake principle permits the archaeologist to see the sequence of deposits in his site as reflecting a relatively dated series of occupations. If the layers are visibly different, the task of sorting them out and formulating a sequence is relatively simple. If the layers cannot be seen with ease, or not at all, the archaeologist hopes that his arbitrary excavation levels will in some way correspond to the deposition levels. By digging in small enough levels, it is probable that more than one level will correspond to a discrete occupation in many cases. Even if this does not hold true, analysis of the excavated materials will show certain changes to occur from the bottom to the top of a deep site representing a series of occupations. While it is not possible to draw sharp lines of division in a case such as this, the general nature of the development and change can be described.

By applying the simple principles of stratigraphy, a long relative sequence can be formulated even when few sites have more than two components. Consider, for example, a river valley in which six different cultures lived over a period of several hundred years. Life in this valley required considerable movement from place to place, so that it was a rare occurrence for a locality to be occupied by more than two of the six societies. Eight sites, each with two components, are excavated in the valley, and each of the eight shows a somewhat different stratigraphy (see Table, next page). We number the six occupations, with number one being the latest and six the earliest. The assemblages from these six occupations are all different from one another, and can be distinguished in all sites where they occur. The first site to be dug shows number three stratified over number five. From this we know that the assemblage typical of three is later than that of five, but we are not certain that number three occurred immediately after number five. The second site shows the later component to be number one, the earlier number six. Numbers one, three, five, and six all differ from each other. We now have two relative sequences of two assemblages each, but we do not know what the relationships between the two sequences are. It is possible that numbers one and six are both earlier or later than numbers three and five. A third site shows number five stratified over number six. From this we can conclude that both one and five are later than six, although number one could be earlier or later than number five. Site four has number four over number six; yet another separate relative sequence. The next four sites to be dug clarify the relationship between all six components. The fifth site has four above five, thus giving us a four-five-six sequence. The sixth site has number two over number three, which is of little help until the seventh site shows number three to overlay number four. This allows us to postulate a two through six relative sequence, and when the eighth site shows number one stratified over number two, the whole sequence of eight components can be dated in a relative series. This relative sequence has been built up in a composite form from a series of eight sites, each with only two stratified components:

SITE	I	II	III	IV	V	VI	VII	VIII	
		1						1	1
						2		2	2
	3					3	3		3
				4	4		4		4
	5		5		5				5
		6	6	6					6

Simple as the basic assumptions of stratigraphy might seem, they are seldom seen in such simplicity and clarity in the field. Many things can distort and confuse the evidence of stratigraphy. Consider, for example, what the results might be of earlier excavation into stratified deposits. If the last occupants of a multicomponent site dug a large hole, perhaps for a house or for a plaza area and piled the earth removed nearby, problems arise if it is in this pile that the archaeologist makes his first excavation. He will find that the top layer, which should be the latest, is in fact the oldest, and the deeper he digs, the later his materials will be. He will be aware of this reversal of the normal stratigraphy only if he digs elsewhere on the site, or if other excavations elsewhere in the area cause him to suspect his results. This type of stratigraphic reversal is rather common and has been a source of error and controversy in a number of cases.

Gophers are disliked not only by gardeners but also by

archaeologists. In some areas of the United States, gopher burrows literally riddle archaeological sites. While gophers cannot completely alter the sequence of stratigraphic deposits, they certainly can blur the picture to a point where it is very difficult to discern the difference between levels. Similar blurring and mixing results from a phenomenon known as *solifluction*. In colder climates, the soil tends to flow and slip during periods of freezing and thawing. Frost heaving, which raises some areas of the ground to higher levels than others, combined with solifluction, can do an excellent job of blending discrete deposits into a rather homogeneous whole.

The idea that archaeological deposits are built up like the layers of a cake frequently does not apply when each component of a site is in a somewhat different location. It is a common occurrence in shell heap sites in California for the lateral or horizontal separation of deposits through time to cause difficulties in stratigraphic interpretation. Such separation probably occurred when a later village was established just beside an earlier one, but not overlapping it. The reasons for such separation were probably many, but could well have included a desire to place a new settlement in an area uncluttered by the trash of previous tenants of the location. If the edges of the levels overlap some sequential arrangement is possible. Often they do not, however, and then the neat layer-cake model is better likened to a cake which has been dropped, its layers slipping apart completely.

While the above problems of stratigraphic interpretation are both real and important, much of the chronology of modern archaeology has derived from the methods of stratigraphy. The massive hill-like city-mounds of the Near East, known as *tells,* are models of stratigraphy in most cases, and the archaeological sequences of this area owe much of their precision to this dating procedure. If any relative method could be thought of as fundamental to the dating of archaeological assemblages over the world, it would be that of stratigraphy.

Seriation

Popularity is a fleeting thing. High tail fins on cars, hula hoops, the twist, all were with us at one time, but have since been replaced by new styles of auto design, toys, and dance steps. If we were to graph the percentage of people in the total population who liked to twist during one-year periods by horizontal bars, higher percentages would produce wider bars. Now, if we arrange these bars in a column representing successive years, the shape created by them, from the introduction of twisting until its replacement by other types of dancing would look rather like a battleship viewed from the air. The beginning would be narrow, like the ship's stern, and as the popularity of twisting grew, the bars would widen, until the height of popularity would be reached amidships, and then the decline in popularity would carry us forward to the bow, narrow like the stern. Similar developmental sequences are followed by most aspects of man's culture; initial small beginnings, growth to maximum popularity, and, finally, small endings. Some sequences last over thousands of years; others persist for centuries, months, or only weeks.

It is this distinctive shape of popularity which makes the method of seriation possible. Seriation is a relative dating method which involves the arrangement of assemblages in such a way that the frequencies of various types of artifacts in them form "battleship-shaped" curves through time.[9] It can allow us to arrange a series of single component sites in relative chronological order in the absence of stratigraphy, and when properly done, it is a technique of considerable value.

An example will show how the archaeologist can use seriation to obtain a relative chronology for a series of sites. A hypothetical tribe, the Cochuma Indians, lived in the Smoky river valley for over five hundred years. Sites marking their villages are found along the banks of the river for a distance of thirty miles. The Cochuma moved their villages every ten to twenty years so that the sites represent short, discrete occupations. During their stay in the Smoky Valley, the Cochuma manufactured three different kinds of pottery: red with white designs, white with black designs, and a gray pottery with incised decoration. Following archaeological tradition,

[9] J. A. Ford, A Quantitative Method for Deriving Cultural Chronology (Washington: Pan American Union, 1962).

these three types of pottery can be called Cochuma White on Red, Cochuma Black on White, and Cochuma Incised. When they first came into the valley, the Cochuma made only Cochuma Incised. About a century later they began to manufacture Cochuma Black on White. As this type grew in popularity, it slowly replaced Cochuma Incised. Later, after Cochuma Incised was no longer made, Cochuma White on Red was invented, and it in turn ultimately replaced Cochuma Black on White. When the Cochuma were driven from the valley by the U. S. Cavalry, they were making only Cochuma White on Red.

When archaeological investigations were carried out in the Smoky Valley, nine sites were excavated. Each was a single component site, and each contained one or more of the Cochuma pottery types. Since many of the other artifacts in the assemblages from the sites were similar, as were the house types and burial customs, the archaeologists were reasonably certain that their sites were all made by the same people but at different times. The nine sites showed the following percentages of the three pottery types:

SITE	COCHUMA INCISED	COCHUMA BLACK/WHITE	COCHUMA WHITE/RED
1	100%	0%	0%
2	0	75	25
3	50	50	0
4	0	0	100
5	0	25	75
6	75	25	0
7	0	100	0
8	0	50	50
9	25	75	0

There is only one possible order in which these nine sites can be arranged which places the three types in a sequence showing gradual increase and decrease. In practice, it is customary to place a graphic presentation of the types on strips of paper, one for each site, with bars representing frequency of types by their width (Fig. 4A). These strips can then be

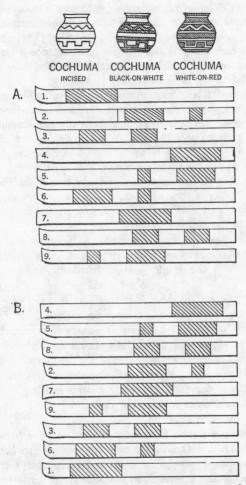

Fig. 4 A. Paper strips arranged according to order of excavation of nine sites. B. Arrangement of paper strips to obtain proper seriation of three pottery types, producing a relative sequence.

placed in different arrangements until one is obtained which produces the proper shape of curves representative of the succession of the three types through time (Fig. 4B). This order is chronological and permits us to arrange a long series of sites, each of which was occupied briefly, in a relative sequence on the basis of pottery popularity.

Note that this technique does not tell us which sites are earlier or later; the sequence as it stands could be interpreted as reflecting the passage of time from site one through four, or four through one. There is also no way of determining how long the entire sequence took to complete. Absolute dates are needed to resolve these problems. This resolution is usually simple, however; absolute dates for any two of the sites indicate the order of the sequence, and dates for the earliest and latest sites, numbers one and four, give us the time span involved in the entire sequence.

Finally, the technique of seriation is based on the assumption that popularity of pottery types and other cultural patterns follows the single peaked "battleship-shaped" curve. That it does is shown by recent studies of colonial gravestone design, where three designs went through cycles of popularity during the eighteenth century in eastern New England, a pattern which can be seen in hundreds of cemeteries.[10] Since gravestones are dated, they permit the archaeologist to check this assumption for accuracy. The three decorative styles form almost perfect "battleship-shaped" curves in their increase and decrease. The early death's heads give way to cherubs, and these in turn are replaced by urn and willow designs by 1800 (Fig. 5).

The term seriation is sometimes used to refer to a somewhat different technique, which frequently also has great value in the relative placement of an assemblage in time. This use of the term refers to the seriation of artifacts on the basis of style change, and is a consideration of the change taking place *within* one of our "battleship-shaped" curves, the change in form of a single series of objects. Seriation of

10 E. S. Dethlefsen and J. Deetz, "Death's Heads, Cherubs and Willow Trees: Experimental Archaeology in Colonial Cemeteries," *American Antiquity,* Vol. 31, No. 4, 1966.

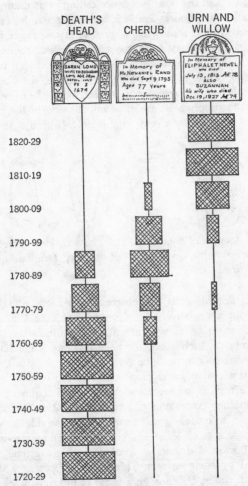

Fig. 5 *Typical stylistic sequence from a New England cemetery (Stoneham, Mass.). The three styles produce nearly perfect curves through time.*

this type, given the term "sequence dating" was used as early as 1902 by Sir Flinders Petrie in arranging a series of Egyptian tombs in a chronological sequence. His arrangement was based on the pottery from the tombs, which could be arranged in such a way that the differences were seen to result from a logical series of changes. For example, the handles of one pot become progressively smaller, until they are finally reduced to simply a painted line on the side in the position formerly occupied by a projecting handle (Fig. 6). Arranging

Fig. 6   A series of pots from Petrie's excavations, showing the progressive reduction in size of handle, terminating in a painted line.

the pots according to the progressive reduction in handle size produces a relatively dated series of objects. While there would seem to be a large measure of intuition involved in such a process, such is actually not so. If one is familiar with his material, he can perceive certain relationships in the decorative style, shape, and proportions, which can be ordered in such a way as to produce a chronological sequence.

For another example of this type of seriation, let us refer once again to colonial gravestones, which provide us with a good measure of chronological control. In the area south and east of Boston, a distinctive local type of gravestone design was used by stone carvers. This design began as a death's head with wings, but through a series of interrelated changes, evolved to a very different series of designs. The period represented by this sequence is one of some sixty years, from 1710 to about 1770 (Fig. 7). The beginning of the sequence involves the reduction of the lower part of the face and the shrinking and final disappearance of the teeth. A heart-shaped design, which appears before the teeth finally vanish, becomes a kind of mouth. Following this change, the feather ends on every other row are reversed in direction, producing a series of wavy lines crossed by arcs surrounding the head. When the arcs are omitted, the wavy lines soon take on the aspect of hair, and this hair goes through a sequence, marked by its becoming more curled and more extensive. The end result is final simplification of the elaborate hair style.

Since this seriation is firmly dated, it is obvious what is taking place in the change in decorative form. When accurate drawings of these designs, without dates, were given to archaeologists to seriate, an order quite similar to that outlined above was formulated, since there is a certain logical way to arrange the designs to achieve the most economical arrangement based on style change. Similar designs are placed adjacent to each other, and order results. Such an approach is basically chronological, and has an application to the problems of achieving a relative chronology.

Radiocarbon dating

Absolute dating has been greatly refined in the past two decades. Before 1948, most absolute dates were obtained by noting the presence in undated sites of objects whose age was known from other associations. For example, Greek pottery, the age of which is known from written historical records in Greece, serves to assign a date to a site on the Black Sea, which has no historical support. Roman coins in England, Mesopotamian seals in India, and Egyptian beads in Europe, all date their final location by a process of extension and cross dating. Such a procedure is quite workable, but is of use only as early as reliable history, not before the fourth millennium B.C. Earlier time stretched into the past and there was little or no way by which the archaeologist could tell how old his sites were.

In 1948 Dr. Willard Libby, then at the University of Chicago, devised a method of absolute dating which has had far-reaching results in archaeology. This method, based on the measurement of the radioactive carbon content of organic materials, is a byproduct of post World War II atomic technology. The workings of radiocarbon dating are simple. Nor-

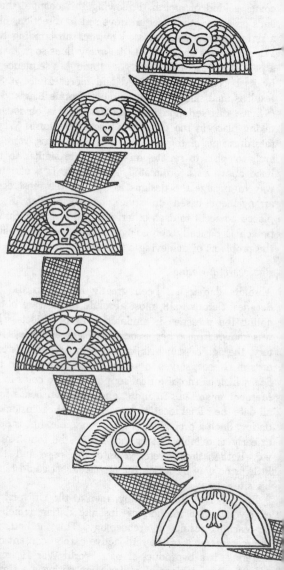

Fig. 7   Seriation of style change in

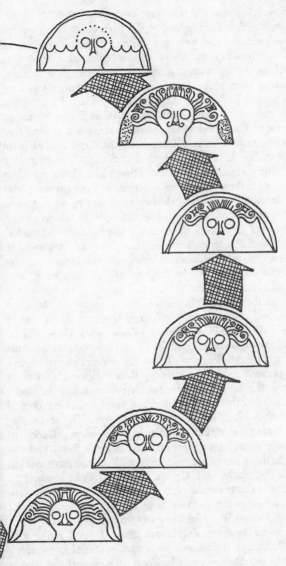

New England gravestone design.

mal, non-radioactive carbon has an atomic weight of 12, which means that the nucleus of the carbon atom has twelve particles—protons and neutrons. The radioactive isotope of carbon (carbon-14) has an additional pair of neutrons in the nucleus. Such an arrangement is unstable, and in time, a carbon-14 atom will radiate the additional neutrons and revert to normal carbon-12. Carbon-14 is produced in the upper atmosphere by the bombardment of nitrogen atoms by cosmic rays. This production is constant, which means that there is a constant ratio of carbon-14 and normal carbon in the atmosphere. Living things, plant and animal, participating in respiratory exchange with the atmosphere, have an identical ratio of carbon-14 to normal carbon in their tissues, maintained through respiration. However, at death, an organism no longer obtains carbon from the atmospheric reservoir, and the amount of carbon-14 in its tissues declines through radiation and reversion to carbon-12. This decay of carbon-14 to carbon-12 occurs at a constant rate; it takes 5730 years for the amount of carbon-14 to drop to half of its former level in a dead organism. This time, 5730 years, is known as the half life of the isotope. In an additional period of the same duration, half of the remaining half of the original amount of carbon-14 will remain, so that in 11,460 years, there will be only one fourth as much carbon-14 as there was at the time the organism died. Since we know the amount of radioactive carbon present in a living thing, it is simply a matter of measuring the amount of radioactivity remaining in wood, shell, bone, or other organic material from an archaeological site, and thus obtaining a date for that site. The measuring is done through a rather complex process of purification of the organic material, converting it to gaseous form, and determining the amount of radiation with a counting device. Theoretically, there will always be some slight amount of radioactive carbon remaining. Practically, in terms of the sensitivity of measuring devices now available, the carbon-14 method of dating is useful to nearly 50,000 years ago.

Error in radiocarbon dating can result from a number of causes. Collecting the sample of organic material from which a date is to be obtained must be done with care. If the sample comes from near the surface of a site, rootlets from living plants on the surface may have grown into it. These must be removed carefully, since if they were to be included with the sample, they might cause contamination which could seriously affect the date obtained, making it more recent than it actually is. It is now thought that carbon-14 dates obtained from shells of marine molluscs must be corrected by adding several hundreds of years, since shellfish incorporate carbonates from sea water which have been essentially removed from the atmospheric reservoir for a long period of time. Great care must also be exercised in the determination of a sample's radioactivity in the laboratory. Samples are usually left in the counter for twenty-four hours or longer to obtain a close estimate of the average counts per minute. The date obtained is usually given with a certain amount of latitude, for example, 2300 plus or minus 200 years old (2300±200). Two thousand three hundred years is the age indicated by the average amount of radioactivity shown by the sample while in the counter, and the latitude expressed is an indication of the degree of variation from the average observed.

Carbon-14 dating provides us with absolute chronological control for the past 50,000 years. Recently, a similar technique based on the reversion of radioactive potassium to argon has been devised. Since the half life of radioactive potassium is much longer than that of carbon (1.3 billion years), this technique provides absolute dates of the order of several millions of years, providing new controls on the absolute age of man on earth.

Dendrochronology

A remarkably precise and ingenious method of absolute dating is based on the annual growth rings of trees. At this time, it is useful only in the southwestern part of the United States, and its use there has produced one of the most precisely dated archaeological sequences anywhere in the world. This method, known as dendrochronology, was devised by an astronomer at the University of Arizona, A. E. Douglass, in 1929, who intended it for use in studying climatic variation in the past. Its application to archaeology was immediately apparent, and it has been a mainstay in southwestern archaeology ever since.

It is common knowledge that a tree adds one ring of new wood each year, and that by counting these, one can determine the age of the tree. These annual rings are not all the same width. Dry years make thin rings; wet years produce wide rings. Measuring the width of each ring in a tree provides a clear picture of the variation of precipitation during the life of the tree. The pattern of alternation of wet and dry seasons over any period of fifty or so years is unique, and not likely to be repeated again in the future. It is this variation and the unique nature of patterning of seasonal rainfall which makes dendrochronology possible.

Dendrochronological dates are obtained by comparing wood samples from archaeological sites with a master chart showing the ring patterns since several centuries B.C. The master chart is obtained through a process of matching the rings of successively older samples of wood. Beginning with a two-hundred-year-old tree cut today, the pattern of ring width variation can be plotted for the past two centuries. A log cut for use in a ranch house constructed in 1850 will match the rings of the first tree for the first hundred or so rings, but if this log was also 200 years old, the two combined provide a continuous sequence of rings back to 1650. By matching a beam cut from a three-hundred-year-old tree for use in a mission church constructed in 1720, we get a master sequence extending to 1420. Such a sequence can then be used to match samples taken from Indian pueblos built in the 1500s from even older trees. By such backward extension, a chart is constructed which extends unbroken into pre-Christian time (Fig. 8). With the master chart a date can be obtained for any structure built during the period covered by it. We simply move the ring pattern back and forth along the master until it matches the corresponding portion of the chart. This then provides us with the date of cutting, and the probable date of the construction of the building from which the sample came. Occasionally, Indians seem to have used beams from older buildings in later construction; such a beam would indicate a date earlier than the construction of the building being dated.

A few simple precautions in the collection of dendrochronological samples insure accuracy. Obviously, the sample must

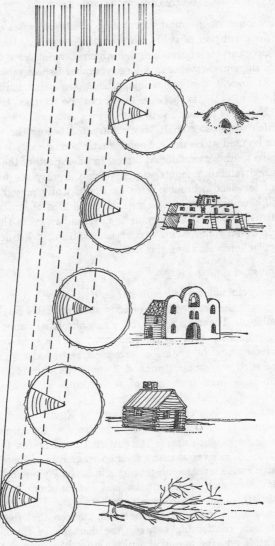

Fig. 8 *Dendrochronological dating: The master tree ring sequence at the top is produced by lapping ring samples from progressively older structures.*

have some of the most recent ring preserved, since without it the exact year of cutting cannot be determined. Usually, it is necessary to collect samples which have at least twenty-five rings preserved, and a larger number is preferable.

At present, dendrochronology has a somewhat limited application. This is because we must be certain that the climate was reasonably the same over the entire area from which the master chart was constructed before the method can be used successfully. Such climatic homogeneity is typical of the southwestern United States. In other parts of the world, annual rainfall amounts vary so widely from place to place that for dendrochronology to be useful many master charts will have to be made, one for each small area of similar rainfall pattern. Such a program is now underway in the Missouri river valley, with master charts being constructed at regular intervals along the river.

Pipe stem dating

Dendrochronology and radiocarbon dating are but two ways in which the archaeologist obtains absolute dates for his assemblage. There is a host of other absolute chronological methods; many of them are quite new, and have not yet been perfected, and others are of extremely restricted application. One such very special method is that which provides accurate dates from fragments of seventeenth- and eighteenth-century English kaolin pipe stems.

Pipes of white clay, manufactured in England and traded to America, are very common in Indian and European colonial archaeological sites in the eastern United States. It is not unusual to recover as many as 2000 fragments of these pipes from a single seventeenth-century site in the Plymouth Colony area; sites such as Jamestown and Williamsburg have produced them in equally great numbers. Jean Harrington, an archaeologist working at Jamestown, noticed that there was a definite relationship between the diameter of the bore of the stem and the age of the pipe. Pipes had been dated on the basis of the shapes of their bowls, but such a method was useless if only stem fragments were available; they are always far more numerous than bowls or whole pipes. Using dated bowls with portions of their stems attached, Harrington discovered that the older the pipe, the larger the bore diameter of the stem. The earliest pipes, dating to about 1600, had stems with bores of 9/64 inch diameter; by 1800, this diameter had decreased to 4/64 inch. This change in diameter probably is due to the fact that pipe stems became longer and thinner during this two-hundred-year period. Using this method of dating, the archaeologist has only to measure the diameter of the bores of the pipe stems from his site, and compare the average bore diameters against a chart which gives the average bore diameters for a number of thirty-year periods. The time periods and average bore diameters are as follows:

DIAMETER	DATES
9/64	1590–1620
8/64	1620–1650
7/64	1650–1680
6/64	1680–1720
5/64	1720–1750
4/64	1750–1800

Suppose we have dug a site in which seventy percent of the stems have a bore diameter of 7/64 inch. Fifteen percent are 6/64 inch, and fifteen percent 8/64 inch. This distribution would suggest that the site was occupied from 1650 to 1680. The few stems in the larger and smaller categories reflect either normal variation in stem diameter, or a slightly longer time of occupation on either end of the period indicated by the majority of the stems. A refinement of this method, using a simple mathematical formula, and yielding a single date which can be thought of as being the middle of the occupation period, has recently been devised by Lewis Binford of the University of California.[11] While the use of pipe stems for dating is only useful in those few sites which produce

11 L. R. Binford, "A New Method of Calculating Dates from Kaolin Pipe Stems," *Southeastern Archaeological Conference Newsletter*, Vol. 9, No. 1, 1961.

them, where it *can* be applied, it is of great value in ordering sites in both a relative and absolute series.

We have discussed but a few of the many methods used by the archaeologist in dating his assemblage. More extensive treatment of the subject can be found in a number of introductory texts treating archaeological method, including those mentioned in the section on excavation.

Chapter III

THE ANALYSIS OF FORM

Artifacts are man-made objects; they are also fossilized ideas. In every clay pot, stone axe, wooden doll, or bone needle, we see preserved what someone once thought pots, axes, dolls, or needles should look like. In every culture, there are conventions which dictate the form of artifacts. We are all familiar with the stereotyped scene in a Western movie in which the hero pulls an arrow from the side of a burning wagon, looks at it, and announces: "Sioux." Not Cheyenne, not Arapaho, but Sioux, and he knows because Sioux arrows look different from those made by other tribes. In all likelihood, a person familiar with arrows made by the different tribes on the American Plains could make such a judgment, and be right. In all their manufactures, the members of a culture have very definite ideas about what makes an object look "right," and how much that object can vary in form until it becomes "wrong." Lila O'Neale, an anthropologist studying the basket making of the Yurok Indians of northern California, discovered the rules of proper basketry among those people by an ingenious technique.[12] She showed pictures of baskets made by many of the women of the tribe to those same women, and invited their criticism. From comments on what was *wrong* with this basket hat or that basket bowl, she was able to outline clearly the limits of variation within which the Yurok thought good baskets were produced.

The mental template

The idea of the proper form of an object exists in the mind of the maker, and when this idea is expressed in tangible form in raw material, an artifact results. The idea is the mental template from which the craftsman makes the object. The form of an artifact is a close approximation of this template, and variations in a group of similar objects reflect variation in

[12] L. M. O'Neale, *Yurok-Karok Basket Weavers* (University of California Publications in American Archaeology and Ethnology, Vol. 32, No. 1); Berkeley, 1932.

the ideas which produce them. What gives form to the idea or mental template held by the maker of an artifact? Certainly tradition, since learning a craft entails the transmission of these templates from generation to generation, and many aspects of them have been present for so long that people simply feel that this shape for an axe or that color for a basket is inherently right. However, factors other than the purely traditional can affect the form of the mental template, and there are other factors which affect the form of the finished product which are completely unrelated to the template involved.

For example, consider the mental template used in the production of a basket made by the Chumash Indians of southern California (Fig. 9). This basket can be described in

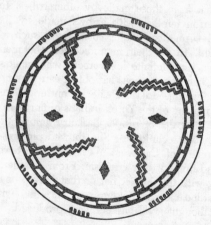

Fig. 9   A typical Chumash basket.

terms of its various *attributes*, discrete features which in their combination give the basket its distinctive form. Obvious attributes include a band of decoration around the inside of the basket near the rim, a mottled dark background color in much of the body, rectilinear stepped patterns, small diamond patterns between the main steps, and a flat circular shape.

Each of these attributes contributes to the form of the basket, and each is present in the basket and was an attribute of the mental template which produced it for a reason. These reasons are not all the same; they could be a matter of technology, function, innovation, or tradition. The band of decoration is present because such bands are a part of the decorative tradition of the Chumash. Only on rare occasions did they make a basket which did not have this decorative band just inside the edge. The rich red-brown mottled background color is the result of the material used to make the basket, a species of rush. The reason for the presence of the band is purely a matter of tradition; the color is the result of a particular technology which employs a specific raw material. Of course, this use of a particular plant is also traditional.

Rectilinear designs are the rule in all basketry since the sewing and weaving techniques used in such manufacture dictate step-like designs. Curved lines can be used, but they are much harder to execute, and are in fact curving sets of angular elements. The diamond patterns between the step designs are unique; the maker used them for the first time when she made this basket. They are a true innovation, and represent a change in the template which was made during the time the basket was being made. Should they have been attractive to other basket makers, they might have been taken into the tradition of the Chumash artists, and would ultimately rank as traditional attributes like the band of decoration. This is one way in which objects change in their form as time passes; new elements are added, old ones removed, and if the modification of the template "takes," the changed pattern becomes an established fact. The shape of the basket, flat and round, is dictated by its function: it is a parching tray, used to roast seeds by tossing them with hot embers.

The mental template for this basket was a combination of a number of attributes; these attributes were present for reasons which were traditional, functional, technological, a matter of innovation, or a function of the materials used. Although the reasons for the selection of the several attributes varied, the product of the template is a distinctive artifact, very similar to others produced by similar templates, and illustrative of a set of ideas shared by the members of the Chumash culture. If we look at baskets made by Indians neighboring the Chumash, we find that they are the products of other idea sets, different templates which are the products of somewhat different factors in their formation.

Some of the variations seen in a set of similar objects—arrowheads, pots, or stone knives—are not the result of slight differences in the mental templates which produced them but of external factors which come into play at the time the object is being made. "Making" a stone arrowhead is really quite different from "making" a clay bowl in a number of ways, and this difference has a lot to do with how accurately the template is translated into stone or clay. Artifacts are the products of technologies which can be divided into two classes, a subtractive class on one hand and an additive class on the other. Subtractive manufacture involves the removal of raw material until the artifact emerges in finished form. In the manufacture of a stone arrowhead, the maker removes sections of the raw material until he has reached a form which approximates the template which he has in mind. In a sense, he extracts the arrowhead from the piece of stone. A woman making a clay pot, on the other hand, is involved in an additive process, building up the clay until the template is expressed to her satisfaction through a process of accumulation. We can view the former process as centrifugal, and the latter as centripetal. The difference between the two processes relates to the accuracy of template expression. Subtractively produced artifacts cannot be repaired in the event the maker slips in the process of manufacture. While flaking a stone knife, if an overlarge flake is removed, there is no way that it can be replaced and removed again in a smaller size. In such a case, the maker must either finish the knife in a form a bit different from that which he intended or discard it and begin anew. If a clay bowl is shaped wrong while being built up, however, it is a simple matter to reshape it to conform more closely to the mental template being expressed. In other words, it is far easier to correct for "goofs" in an additive process than in a subtractive process.

A fascinating result of this difference between the two processes is that errors which occur in the process of material removal are likely to be preserved archaeologically, while errors which occur during an additive process, if corrected, are destroyed by the correction, and are not preserved. One would then expect a greater amount of variation resulting from error, and not template variation, in those artifacts which are made subtractively, than in those made by an additive technology.

What has all this to do with archaeology? In the process of studying the form of the artifacts which he has excavated, the archaeologist is deeply concerned with how these artifacts vary and how they can best be classified according to their form to aid him in his interpretations. We have seen that variation in the form of artifacts is a complex thing, and that the causes for this variation are many. Variation in objects which reflects template variation is quite relevant to understanding the culture of their makers, while variation introduced by problems of technology may not be germane to cultural reconstruction.

The type concept

The most frequently applied concept in the study of form is that of the artifact type. The type concept is central to formal analysis, and it has been a most useful tool to the archaeologist. It has also been criticized considerably, and, while some of the criticism might be justified, much of it results from expecting too much from its application or from using it to answer questions for which it is ill suited.

To understand exactly what the type concept is, and how it is applied, let us watch an archaeologist at work in his laboratory. He has brought all the fragments of pottery (sherds) from one component of his site to a long table, and begins to sort them according to obvious similarities. Three piles begin to emerge. One is made up of sherds which are painted in black on a white ground color. A second pile is of sherds which are plain gray in color, with no decoration. The third is made up of sherds which are yellow with red painted decoration. Tentatively then, he has isolated three types in his pottery. Upon closer inspection of one of the piles, that of black on white painted sherds, he discovers that it can be subdivided into a group of sherds which have designs painted solid black and a second group with black fine line painting. His other two groups subdivide in a similar manner: some yellow sherds have curvilinear designs, others rectilinear decoration, and the plain gray is made up of very thin sherds on the one hand and quite thick ones on the other. He proceeds to make this division in each class and now has six groups.

In addition to these six piles, he also has two very small groups of a few sherds each. One group has black designs on a yellow background; the other has red designs on a white ground color. These sherds fall between the chairs of his tentative groups. He is faced with the choice of considering them as two additional types of equal status with the other six or of thinking of them as not belonging to the universe of pottery which is typical of his site. Either explanation is possible. Remembering the pattern formed by changing styles (explained in the discussion of seriation), he might consider them to be minor types, which were more popular earlier or later than the time represented by the pottery which he is classifying. On the other hand, red on white and black on yellow pottery might have been popular at other sites occupied at the same time, and the pottery from these sites might contain only small amounts of black on white and red on yellow pottery. In this case, the presence of these "oddballs" might be explained by the trading of pottery between contemporary villages. These problems can only be resolved by comparing the pottery from his site with the pottery from other sites of the same and different time periods.

A third possibility will present itself to the archaeologist as he builds his typology. Perhaps the red on white and black on yellow pottery represents the extremes of variation within the pottery made at the time. Those red and black and black and yellow pots may have been thought of as not quite proper by the people who made all the pottery now being sorted. If so, the archaeologist can simply relegate the two small groups to a category which he believes to reflect the extreme of variation from the norms of pottery manufacture which were applied by the people who were making the more usual black on white and red on yellow types. This brings us to an important point. When the archaeologist has sorted his pottery into groups which meet with his satisfaction, he will have selected one of a number of possible orderings of the material. If another archaeologist were to sort the same pottery but use different attributes as sorting criteria, he might produce very different groups. For example, should this second sorting proceed according to the shape of the lip of the pot in cross section and the color of the clay inside the sherd, black on white sherds might well be mixed with red on yellow ones, and even plain gray ones. The "odd" sherds might be "normal" according to this classification. Nevertheless, if in his published report the archaeologist describes the attributes which he used to define one or another type, any other worker who is classifying similar pottery can repeat the sorting process, and thus make his pottery comparable with that previously described.

Furthermore, by selecting common and obvious attributes and stating the observed variation in these attributes in his published description of a type, the archaeologist is describing some of the dimensions of variation in the templates which produced the pottery. It matters little if his attributes were selected arbitrarily, as long as they are prevalent enough in his collection to allow him to create usable groups.

An artifact type description is, therefore, a statement of a set of somewhat variable attributes which can be observed to occur together in the majority of cases.[13] It is the creation of the archaeologist and not necessarily of the makers of the artifacts being analyzed. Often the question is asked, "Do types reflect ideas held by the makers of the objects being typed, or are they arbitrary?" Such a question is largely irrelevant. One purpose of creating types is to order the artifacts from a site in such a way as to permit comparison with artifacts from other sites. It may well be that some types are almost perfect descriptions of the templates responsible for them; whether this is true or not in no way interferes with the main aim of typology, that of classification which permits comparison.

Such comparison allows the archaeologist to align his assemblage with others in time and space. In the construction

---

[13] In actual practice, types are defined according to more than a single attribute; the example given is oversimplified for the sake of clarity. For a typical description of a type, see Appendix.

of relative sequences equivalent components of different sites are equated by observing typological similarities between their artifacts. Comparison with assemblages which are earlier and later permits seriational chronology and the construction of sequences in this manner. Neither spatial alignment nor seriation could be easily done in the absence of typology. As long as the descriptions of types are lucid and sufficiently detailed, archaeologists can bring about order in the arrangement of sites and components in time and space. It matters little how fine a division is made of an assemblage in the course of classification. The same group of similar artifacts could be divided into ten types or two, depending on how specific the archaeologist who classified it was. Since such classifications are arbitrary, no violence is done to cultural reality. As long as this is kept in mind, types serve admirably in the spatial and temporal ordering of archaeological materials. Further interpretation is not possible until such order is first established. When the control of the variables of time and space has been achieved, the archaeologist can proceed to study his material in primarily cultural terms.

Chapter IV

SPACE AND TIME

To the average person, the expression "space-time" probably suggests either science fiction, physics, or astronomy. To the archaeologist, space and time, along with form, are vital dimensions of archaeological data. We have seen how order is brought to the formal dimension of an assemblage through the application of typology; the dimension of space is ordered by the location of the sites which produced it and other assemblages, and its place in the stream of time is fixed by a number of chronological methods.

In archaeological thinking, space and time are often pictured as forming a block. We can imagine this block as a cube in which space is represented by the length and width and time by the depth. The bottom of the cube is the earliest in time, the top the latest. Such a cube is "cut" from a larger area, representing a longer time (ultimately the world, and all of time since man first appeared nearly two million years ago), but cultural process in the space within such a cube can be represented by measurable forms.

An example will make this analogy clear (Fig. 10). Supposing that, in A.D. 1400, a new and much improved type of bronze axe was invented in one village. Its advantages were immediately apparent, and soon other villages were learning about and making the new type of axe. As the knowledge spread, the distribution of the axe could be seen to form a circle when plotted on a map. The diameter of this circle grew as time passed; ten miles in 1410, twenty miles in 1420, thirty miles in 1430, until by 1450, the villages within a circular area fifty miles in diameter were making and using the new tool. The shape created by the distribution of this new axe at any point in time is circular, but in time *and* space it is that of a cone. As the area of the axe's use grew in extent, time passed, so that larger circles were formed as the top of our cube was approached along the dimension of time.

A perfect cone would be formed in this manner only if all rates were constant. Variations in the time needed for the

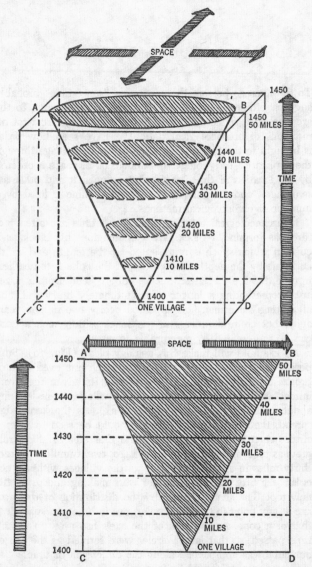

Fig. 10 *The formation of cones and triangles in space and time.*

knowledge to move from one village to another, geographical barriers, or a reluctance on the part of some people to adopt the new axe would distort the shape of the cone, giving it bulges and dents, although the general shape would prevail.

How does knowing about this shape help us in understanding events and developments in the past? Archaeologists make use of the form of the space-time distributions of their data to learn about things past as general as the movement of a new technology across a continent and as specific as the movement of a single people along a river. In practice, they look at the distribution of archaeological data in space and time in two dimensions. This form can be imagined by picturing the result of cutting our cube in half parallel to the time dimension, at right angles to the spatial plane. Our cone now appears as a triangle, with the base at the top and the apex at the bottom (Fig. 10). Triangular shapes of this type are obtained by plotting the space-time coordinates of archaeological data in our two dimensional space.

Let us consider as an example the introduction of farming in the Near East and Europe. This event was a major one since it allowed man to control his food supply for the first time in such a way that he could better insure an ample larder at all times. A whole set of cultural changes accompanied this invention: larger villages, settled life free of the uncertainties of hunting as the only source of food, and ultimately, cities and civilization based on the very productive economy made possible by agriculture.

Obviously archaeologists have been quite interested in the date and nature of the spread of the knowledge of farming. Archaeological evidence of farming is diverse; not only are the remains of grains and other food plants often found, but farming implements and large sites also indicate the practice. Sites yielding such evidence are found over Europe and the Near East. It is now believed that the earliest farmers lived somewhere in the Near East in the area between Anatolia and northern Iraq in the eighth millennium B.C. From here, farming spread into Europe until it reached the North Sea area between 4000 and 3500 B.C.

Figure 11 shows a map of Europe and the Near East, and the earliest dates of farming at each of several points. The

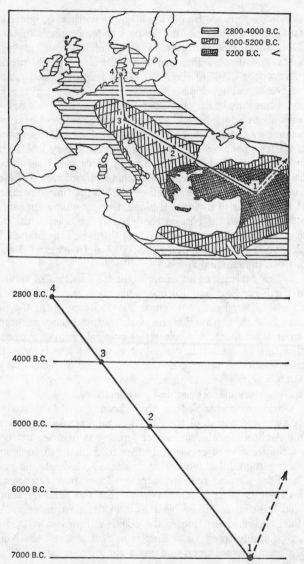

Fig. 11 *The diffusion of the Neolithic in Central Europe.*

space-time chart below the map represents a line connecting these points as the space dimension, and the period between 7000 and 2800 B.C. as the time dimension. By plotting the several locations in space and time, a line is formed which corresponds to one side of the triangle shape described above. The other side of the triangle would be formed in another direction away from the Near Eastern center. We should note two things about this chart. The spread of agriculture is indicated by the slope of the line; movement in such a diagram is always "uphill" in time. The rate of this movement is indicated by the steepness of the slope, with steeper slopes indicating slower rates. Such slopes can never reach the horizontal, since this would represent instantaneous appearance of the trait at a number of points.

Horizon and tradition

In broader context, the form of lines of this type is the basis of two important archaeological concepts, those of *horizon* and *tradition*.[14] The concept of an archaeological horizon is that of a set of traits which links a number of cultures over a broad area in a short time. In the Peruvian area a widespread art and architectural style, known as Chavín, appears at about 800 B.C. It is characterized by feline and condor motifs in the decoration of ceramics and architectural stonework (Fig. 12). Plotting the space-time distribution of sites containing Chavín type objects makes it clear that the spread of the ideas responsible for the style was rapid; the slope of the space-time line is quite shallow. This manifestation is known as the Chavín Horizon, and its peculiar space-time pattern suggests certain things about it. It moved rapidly over a large area. Therefore it must have had considerable pressure behind it. What types of cultural processes are known to accelerate the spread of ideas over large areas, and among different peoples? The most likely possibilities are religious missionization and conquest by force. Since the Chavín style seems in some way linked with the ritual aspects of early

[14] These concepts are fully developed in G. R. Willey and P. Phillips, *Method and Theory in American Archeology* (Chicago: University of Chicago Press, Phoenix Books, 1962).

Fig. 12   A stela carved in Chavín style.

Peru, as imperfectly as they are known, and since there is little evidence of conflict or fortification at the time, the Chavín horizon can be thought of as reflecting some type of cult spread. In fact, the term Chavín Cult has been used to describe it. When the Spanish arrived in Peru in the sixteenth century, a horizon (Inca) was well along in the process of forming, this time spread through planned conquest by the Inca state.

In contrast to the horizon concept, that of tradition is marked by a long temporal duration with relatively little spatial extent. The tradition is a configuration of traits which has a very long life. Plotted in a space-time block, traditions would have very steep slopes. An excellent example of a tradition is provided by the painting of pottery in black on white designs in the American Southwest. This type of decoration is a hallmark of southwestern ceramics over a period of more than a thousand years, although it is limited to a small area centering on the "four corners" area of Colorado, Utah, Arizona, and New Mexico.

Both concepts are to some extent arbitrary segments of the fluid continua of space and time. Reduced to an absurdity, one might say that horizons are thin traditions of wide distribution, or that traditions are limited horizons of long duration. This may seem as ridiculous as the idea of the world's largest midget, or smallest giant, but it makes and underscores the point that there should be no fixed dimensions for either horizon or tradition. In fact, most space-time patterns formed by archaeological materials are neither in the true sense, since they are distributed in both dimensions to a considerable extent. The concepts of horizon and tradition are usually reserved for clear instances of extreme dimensions of time or space, usually if not always linking several cultures, and of use at the broadest level of archaeological integration.

Space-time slope patterns

On a more discrete scale, the pattern of sloping lines in space and time tells us about more specific happenings than those affecting continents over thousands of years. At this level, the classifications made by the archaeologist of his artifacts become more important.

A rather complex example from the Missouri river valley will serve to show how space-time slopes, problems of typology, and the shifts in popularity which underlay seriation combine to tell the archaeologist about a people. Although this example is based on archaeological fact, it has been simplified and somewhat schematized for the sake of clarity of presentation. We can first tabulate the data involved; these are the "knowns" of the case.

Location: the Missouri River, between the White and Cheyenne rivers, South Dakota (Fig. 12).

Time: between 1700 and 1800. All sites contain trade material obtained from Europeans: beads, guns, wire, iron knives.

Sites: remains of many villages which had been composed of earth-covered lodges, located on the terraces above the flood plain of the Missouri River.

Culture: in this case, accounts of early travelers in the area tell us that the people involved were the Arikara Indians, a tribe who farmed the river bottoms and hunted bison on the open plains.

When the first sites in this area were dug, in the early 1950s, most artifact types were quite similar from site to site, particularly those of stone and bone. Typological classifications constructed from one site were applicable to the others. In the case of pottery, however, two distinct types emerged from the classifications. Each was identified primarily by the cross-sectional shape of the lip, square in one case, and "braced" in the other, the latter being the result of applying a rolled strip of clay around the rim of the pot. Except for this difference, the types were similar. The former square lip form was designated Talking Crow Ware, the latter, Stanley Ware, and each was divided into a number of subtypes. Subtypes of Talking Crow Ware were similar to those of Stanley Ware except for lip treatment.

Two of the first sites excavated had very different amounts of each of the two types. The first, located in the southern end of the area, had almost all Talking Crow Ware with small amounts of Stanley, while the other, a hundred odd miles to the north, had mostly Stanley Ware, with a few sherds of Talking Crow. What was the most reasonable explanation of these differences? Might not the presence of the minority type in each site indicate trade between contemporary villages along the river? Or were the sites of different dates, and the differences in ceramics a matter of separation in time, with one type replacing the other? At the time these first sites were dug, one couldn't be certain. However, with the excavation of more village sites between the first two, two things became apparent. First, the evidence of stratigraphy, and of placing house floors from different sites in a sequence based on a progressive change in their size, strongly indicated an upward slope of the line marking the latest date of occupation of the area by the Arikara. The slope was upwards in an upstream direction; it suggested a northward movement of some influence causing the Arikara to abandon their villages. Since this slope marked the last occupation of sites, rather than specific traits within the sites, the inference was that the Arikara were moving as a people up the river, arriving later further upstream, and staying later. Second, if Talking Crow and Stanley Wares were used to seriate those sites containing European materials, the seriational order agreed with the slope and sequence dating of house sizes. With this additional information, it seemed probable that Talking Crow Ware actually became Stanley Ware as the Arikara moved slowly upstream. From this we can see the relationships between space, time, and form in archaeology.

This example clearly demonstrates that the arbitrary classification of pottery into two types still achieved certain useful purposes. In those cases where both types were present, the classifiers were sharply dividing a shaded continuum. At the extreme ends of the area, there are sites which produce only Stanley Ware or only Talking Crow Ware. Yet the description of the types and their use in seriation allowed certain inferences regarding the movement of the Arikara along the Missouri River. The combined pattern of slope and type change is shown in Figure 13.

We might ask: "Did this exercise actually tell us much about the Arikara as a culture?" The answer is: "No." But we should also remember that typology is an integrative procedure and not an inferential one. We did determine an

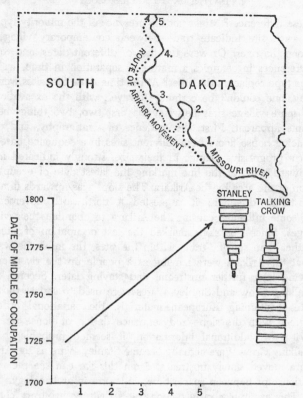

Fig. 13   Pottery change and population movement.

aspect of a people's movement from place to place; we shall see that, in another context, this is a useful thing to know.

Leaving aside for the moment the dimension of time, there are certain aspects of the dimension of space to consider. The distribution of artifacts of identical or similar types in a contiguous area usually permits the archaeologist to draw a line around an area within which a pool of shared ideas probably once existed. In a sense, a culture is such an idea pool, and spatial units of this type probably correspond in many cases to discrete cultures in the past. Certain cautions must accompany such a statement; there are numerous cases of very different cultures sharing in virtually identical artifact types, as well as instances of the same culture manifesting itself in its tangible products in a number of ways. If such configurations of shared types do not demand identification as the cultures of the past, they are at least the criteria whereby most archaeological "cultures" are identified; the Danubian culture of Europe, the Anasazi culture of Colorado, the Moche culture of Peru, the Maya culture of Guatemala, and the Wilton culture of South Africa being but five of literally thousands known today.

Chapter V

CONTEXT

Grid systems, labeled bags, careful mapping, the recording of features and strata, all these field techniques insure that the artifacts can be related to the site and to each other in an accurate way which will permit the archaeologist to describe the nature of the *associations* in his site. The circumstances of occurrence of archaeological data tell us much about the people who lived on the site. The contextual aspect of archaeological material is one of the most obvious clues to past behavior, and one of the few which is often apparent while in the field.

It is hardly necessary to cite extensive examples of this type of inference in its simplest application; a little imagination provides us with any number of instances which might exist and illustrate the value of archaeological association. The discovery of bones representing joints of meat in a burial suggests an offering of food, perhaps for the use of the deceased in his long journey. Numbers of flint scrapers and spear points found with a mass of bison bones at the base of a high cliff on the western plains is clear evidence of butchering animals killed by stampeding them over the brink. Cow ribs, smoothed on one edge, and found on the floor of a vat used for soaking hides preparatory to tanning at a California mission were probably used for scraping the hair from the lime-soaked hides.

By piecing together individual instances of such associations from a single site, we ultimately get an impression of the use of a number of objects and also of the location of such activities. There are other aspects of context which go beyond those simply involving single objects in single locations. An interesting artifact commonly found in the mountainous areas of California is the bedrock mortar. Bedrock mortars are cylindrical holes in outcroppings of bedrock and were used with stone pestles for pounding acorns into a mush for food. Since these mortars are a part of an immovable mass of rock, they could not be carried about. They occur in groups scattered throughout wide areas. In one sense, such a group could be considered a site, made up of a single type of artifact. The context of these mortar concentrations in terms of the environment is instructive in understanding certain aspects of the economic behavior of California Indians. They are frequently found in the vicinity of extensive stands of oak trees. In most cases, there is no cultural debris in the vicinity of these mortars. It would seem that they were grinding stations used by the Indians for milling their acorns on the spot, prior to transporting the acorn flour back to their villages. The peculiar context of bedrock mortars permits such an inference. We know from historical accounts of California Indians that they were somewhat mobile, particularly during the summer months when they moved through the mountains in search of ample stands of oak from which they might harvest acorns. There are numerous sites representing such small groups of Indians in the mountain country. When these sites are excavated, large stone mortars, probably used for the same purpose as those in bedrock, are found. At times, these weigh as much as a hundred pounds or more. In view of the context of the bedrock mortars, these large fully shaped mortars might not have been carried away when the group moved on, but simply left behind for use at another time. A hundred-pound stone mortar is hardly an object that a mobile group of people would want to transport from spot to spot, and chances were probably excellent that they would be there when the people returned. Thus the context of both bedrock and carved stone mortars suggests periodic use by the same or even different groups of people.

The non-artifactual context of an assemblage frequently provides us with information regarding past behavior. Analysis of the remains of plants and animals in a site sheds light on the food habits and preferences of its former inhabitants, as well as the available resources at the time. The reconstruction of this aspect of past cultures provides us with information concerning the utilization of various resources by the people, and can even permit the reconstruction of specific practices. This segment of archaeology almost always requires the help of botanists and zoologists trained in identifying such remains.

In the cellars of the seventeenth-century Pilgrims of Plymouth Colony large quantities of pig bones have been found. The remains of pig so outnumber those of other food animals, that we are almost tempted to suggest that the first Thanksgiving may have consisted of roast pork rather than turkey. Pigs probably served as a basic food animal quite well, since they can run free in the forest, and their flesh can be preserved by a number of smoking and salting processes which require no cold storage.

A most useful technique for providing another dimension to the non-artifactual context of an archaeological assemblage is that of pollen analysis. Pollen preserves well in the ground, and can be identified as to the species of plant which produced it by microscopic analysis. Even if few actual plant remains are found, pollen grains frequently tell us something about the plants which were present at the time, including those known to have been under domestication. The study of pollen has provided a dramatic demonstration of the introduction of farming into Central and Northern Europe. Early agriculture in this area was practiced by a method known as slash and burn, which entailed the burning off of the forest cover, planting the land thus cleared and enriched by the ash, and using it until its fertility had been largely reduced. When such a plot no longer produced a good yield, another would be cleared by burning, and the old plot would return to a growth of grass. Pollen "profiles," made up by identifying the pollen from layer to layer in sites in the area, show this sequence clearly. The lowermost levels have pollen of forest trees, followed at times by a thin layer of charcoal representing the burning of a plot in the vicinity. Atop this charcoal layer is found the pollen of domesticated plants, and finally the pollen of wild grasses, showing the abandonment of the plot and its reversion to grass cover. This sequence of pollen succession provides a useful context in which to understand better the assemblages of the first farmers of Central and Northern Europe.

Slash and burn farming is a specific technique associated with the cultivation of plants, reconstructed by the identification of their pollen. The butchering techniques of a group of prehistoric South Dakota Indians has been reconstructed

through the study of animal bones. By identifying all the
bison bones from a site occupied in A.D. 1400 and determining
how they had been broken and cut, it was possible to describe exactly how the animal had been butchered and to
determine that this butchering had not all been done in the
village, since certain bones were not found there, having been
left at the location where the bison had been cut apart.[15] The
identification of animal bone according to age can sometimes
tell us the time of the year a certain site was occupied, since
large numbers of bones of very young animals indicate occu-
pancy during the spring and early summer months. In a similar manner, the identification of bones of migratory birds and
fish can place the season of occupation of a site with considerable precision, and both approaches are quite useful if we
are concerned with determining whether sites were occupied during the entire year or only seasonally. Seasonal occupation suggests greater mobility than does year-round use,
and mobility of this type suggests a somewhat different cultural system from that of permanent peoples.

The contextual aspect of an archaeological assemblage is
an extremely valuable aid to inference; it is also very easily
destroyed by incorrect excavation procedure. The critical
operations of ample recording, careful exposure of artifacts
and features, and precise cataloguing insure its preservation.
It has often been said that sites are artifacts which are destroyed in the process of field work; such a statement contains
a large measure of truth. In many ways, the associations of
the data are more precious than the assemblage itself. An
artifact with no information concerning location and associations is of little value. If is for this reason above all others
that amateurs are discouraged from digging sites. Even those
lay archaeologists who have adequate training in field techniques cannot do a complete job unless they are also trained
in general anthropological theory, since archaeological materials must be excavated and interpreted in anthropological

[15] T. E. White, "Butchering Techniques at the Dodd and Phillips
Ranch Sites" in D. J. Lehmer, *Archaeological Investigations in the
Oahe Dam Area, South Dakota, 1950–51* (Smithsonian Institution,
Bureau of American Ethnology, Bulletin No. 158); Washington,
1954.

terms. If such non-professional activity is potentially dangerous, reckless digging for the sake of obtaining a collection of "relics" must be universally condemned. Such collections, literally torn from their context in the site, can tell us little or nothing about the culture responsible for their existence.

Among professional archaeologists, there has been a slow development in the strategy of excavation which reflects an increasing awareness of the value of complete contextual inference. In the early days of archaeological field work, it was customary to make deep and narrow excavations into sites, a practice aimed primarily at the construction of developmental sequences and the explication of the outlines of culture history. The second aim of archaeology, the discovery of the functioning of cultural systems at single points in time, was not served too well by such an approach. Modern archaeology is characterized by extensive exposure of single components, a technique which allows us to see the contextual aspect of an assemblage in great detail. This approach has been in use for years, but has recently been re-emphasized, with exciting results. At the site of Ambrona in Spain, careful excavation of a large area revealed the remains of many animals, including large elephants, which had been butchered, associated with tools and fireplaces left there by man over three hundred thousand years ago.[16] Such a pattern of associations, requiring the exposure and careful mapping of large areas representing contemporary activity in the past, when combined with deep sequence-oriented excavation, combine to tell the archaeologist about activities in detail, as well as changes in them through time. In each case, the context of the assemblages is of critical importance to the proper execution of the job.

[16] See F. C. Howell, *Early Man* (New York: Life Nature Library, Time, Inc., 1965), pp. 88–89.

Chapter VI

FUNCTION

Take a glass coffeepot, a set of rosary beads, a wedding ring, a fishing pole complete with reel, a jewelry box, a pair of skis, an eight ball from a pool table, a crystal chandelier, a magnifying glass, a harmonica, and a vacuum tube and break them to pieces with a hammer. Bury them for three centuries, and then dig them up and present them to a literate citizen of Peking. Could he tell you the function of the objects which these fragments represent? A slightly far-fetched situation, we might say, but in many ways, this is exactly the problem facing the archaeologist who is attempting to determine the function of the various artifacts in his assemblage.

Even if our highly educated Chinese gentleman were able to identify the objects in terms of form—a glass container with a lid, some beads which had been strung together, a ring for the finger—he would still have difficulty determining that the pot was for coffee, that the ring signified the social and religious custom of marriage, or that the beads served to keep a tally of prayers. Could we do better with a similarly treated set of objects from modern China?

Function is a many-faceted aspect of artifacts. The same artifact might have served a number of functions, some simultaneously, in the culture of its origin, and the archaeologist must at least be aware of the difficulties inherent in assigning a function to a piece of *something*.[17] Not that this is an impossible task, since many of the artifacts which are routinely encountered indicate something of their function in an obvious way. The explicit functional aspect of artifacts is determined by their form and by their contextual aspect in many cases.

In the case of single artifacts, it is safe to say that almost all functional identifications are a matter of analogy with known cases. We know that an arrowhead served a certain

17 Various aspects of artifact function are discussed in L. R. Binford, "Archaeology as Anthropology," *American Antiquity*, Vol. 28, No. 4, 1962.

function because we have seen similar objects with the same use where it could be determined. Pots are obviously containers, are they not? We even use them on our kitchen ranges, and for serving at the dinner table. Some of the analogies which archaeologists employ in their functional labeling of artifacts come from our own culture, but others are seen in cultural contexts quite different from that of twentieth-century America. For this reason, archaeologists benefit greatly from what anthropology tells them about other life ways around the world. For example, in sites in the Amazon river valley, numerous sharpened stones are found. If the archaeologist did not know that such stones are used today set into wood for grating manioc, a root crop used by the Amazonian Indians, he would not be able to ascribe this function to the stones, and infer manioc grating in the past.

Another avenue to the understanding of the function of certain artifacts is through what has been called the imitative experiment.[18] This approach consists of attempting to use the objects in question in the same way they are thought to have been used in the past, and observing their efficiency. If the artifact involved was used for cutting, such experimentation would include its use in the supposed manner, and the pattern of wear on the cutting edge might be observed to determine if it resembles that already present.

While both analogy and imitation offer avenues to the functional assessment of an artifact, there are certain dangers involved. By analogy with other cultures we frequently suggest that highly decorated objects such as baskets and pots were used for very special purposes, and that strictly utilitarian artifacts are usually not the objects of great artistic elaboration. Now in many instances this is true, and the assignment of plain, undecorated potsherds to a utilitarian class of pottery is probably safe in the majority of cases. Yet Lila O'Neale's study of Yurok and Karok basketry shows a very different set of reasons for the particular type of design which is placed on baskets. The Yurok and Karok make baskets for cooking—mush bowls as they are called—and also "fancy

[18] R. Ascher, "Experimental Archaeology," *American Anthropologist*, Vol. 63, No. 4, 1961.

baskets" as gifts, hats, and for storing valuables. Fancy baskets have complex designs, while mush bowls have relatively simple decoration. When asked why fancy designs were not used on mush bowls, the answer given was that such designs, while actually easy to execute in many cases, involved frequent cutting and insertion of decorative materials, and that such a process made the basket liable to leaking, and therefore ill suited for cooking purposes. It turns out that while cooking baskets are decorated in "simple" designs, they are in fact the more difficult to execute in many cases, because of the complex counting system required for stitch setting for these motifs. While complexity of decoration certainly correlates with special purpose use in this case, it is certainly not because the makers believed their cooking bowls not worthy of great artistic effort. This example stresses the important fact that any part of a culture must be viewed in terms of the whole cultural pattern. Even if they are virtually identical in form, baskets of culture A are not necessarily comparable to those of culture B, in terms of the way they are thought of by the members of the culture. This is a most important consideration in using analogy for functional identification.

When analogy breaks down, through the artifact's being totally unfamiliar, functional identification of an individual object encounters a formidable barrier. It is a matter of mild joking that all those artifacts which archaeologists cannot identify are automatically classified as "ceremonial objects." A joke, perhaps, but uncomfortably true in many cases. Whether certain cigar-shaped polished stone objects, known as charm stones in California where they are found, are ceremonial objects or served some purpose forever unknown, is absolutely moot. Almost all sites produce such enigmatic objects, and when context, analogy, and imitation fail, little more can be done to clarify their function in the past.

Usually, portions of assemblages will suggest certain broad functions even when all the artifacts within them cannot be assigned specific functional designations. One way in which assemblages are frequently classified is by functional categories. In this way, the archaeologist groups those artifacts relating to subsistence, ritual, warfare, transportation, housing, and other similar sets. The contextual aspect of the artifacts is of considerable help in this case, since grouped associations suggest some common function for such artifact groups.

Entire assemblages can be thought of as having a functional aspect as well. A site which produces a long series of arrowheads, knives, and spear points associated with large quantities of animal bone clearly suggests the functional aspect of the assemblage to be that of serving its makers in the pursuit of hunting as the major economic basis for their culture. In contrast, an assemblage with pottery, agricultural implements, the remains of permanent houses, and quantities of charred grains clearly functioned as a means to the end of farming for its owners, a lifeway quite different from the former.

It can be seen that the determination of function is at the same time a potentially difficult and important archaeological goal. That it has been done with considerable success and imagination can be seen by reading any of the excellent reports written by archaeologists on their sites, a number of which are listed in the Bibliography of this book.

Chapter VII

STRUCTURE

In its simplest application, the formal analysis of artifacts places them into categories based on shared attributes. The end result of typology is the creation of groups of similar artifacts. We have seen that such a process implicitly recognizes a patterning of behavior on the part of the makers of the artifacts, although the types do not necessarily correspond to groups they would perceive as different. Since the set of ideas and actions responsible for the creation of the object and its mental template derive from a variety of sources—traditional, functional, technological, innovative—some further standardization must have prevailed to produce a series of artifacts which share not only in their attributes, but also in the way those attributes were combined. In other words, the whole is more than the sum of its parts, and while formal analysis concentrates on the parts, the structural aspect of an artifact reflects the rules which govern the combination of these attributes.

In anthropology, the idea of structural rules is most strongly developed in the area of linguistics, the study of language. Linguists have been as deeply concerned with the structure of language as with its content and function. The branch of linguistics which concerns itself with the structural aspect of language is known as structural linguistics. Linguists have defined a set of units which form the structural basis of all languages and, through the study of these units, have been able to demonstrate how different languages combine sounds into functional communication systems.

The two basic units of the structure of language are the *phoneme* and the *morpheme*. A general understanding of the concepts of the phoneme and morpheme will help us in understanding the structural aspect of archaeological data. The phoneme can be defined as a class of sounds which affects the meaning of words. Consider the words *bat* and *hat*. These mean totally different things in English, and differ in only one respect, the initial sound. In a similar way, *hat* and *hot* have different meanings, differing only in the medial sound, and *hat* and *had* differ only in the final sound. Such minimal sounds are considered phonemes when they affect the meaning of the word, and two words that differ only in one phoneme form what is called a *minimal pair*. *Bat* is a single word made up of three phonemes, *b*, *a*, and *t*. Note that we are concerned only with sound; the written form of a word has no direct one-to-one relationship to its phonemic structure. Thus while *beat* and *beet* are written differently, they are made up of the same three phonemes. The phoneme of the long *e* sound can be written in a number of ways; consider the words *key, quay, receive, believe, subpoena, seek, Caesar, steam, elite,* and *cede,* all of which contain the long *e* phoneme, but written in ten different ways. For their written recording of a language, linguists have a set of standard symbols to indicate sounds, one symbol for each phoneme.

The phoneme is therefore the minimal structural unit of sound which affects meaning. We have said that it is a *class* of sounds, however. This is so since no two persons give precisely the same sound to any phoneme; dialect differences, slight differences in the anatomy of the speech producing organs, and individual variations in speech create such differences. But while one person might pronounce *pin* with a breath of air following the *p* sound, and another will not aspirate it in this manner, these minor variations do not change the meaning of the word *pin* in each case. There are instances, to be sure, where the distinction seems phonemic to some listeners. Certain people from the South pronounce *pin* and *pen* almost identically, using forms of the *e* and *i* sound in each word which are very similar. Phonemes are therefore classes of variable sounds which have the same effect on the meaning of a word. The individual variation of a given phoneme, nasalized and non-nasalized *a* sounds for example, are called allophones.

Phonemes can only be defined for specific languages, and the phonemes for one language are not necessarily those of another. Differences which are merely allophonic in English are phonemic in some American Indian languages.

The morpheme is a class of sounds which carries meaning.

Consider the word *house*, for example. This sound has a specific meaning in English, and it cannot be reduced to lesser structural units without destroying that meaning. Change the initial *h* phoneme to an *m* phoneme, and another morpheme results. Is *houses* a single morpheme? It isn't, since there are two sounds which convey meaning in this case, *house* and *es*. Now if we were looking at a housing subdivision with a friend, and said to him, while pointing at the houses, *"es!,"* the sound would not have the meaning of plurality unless it was attached to the word *house*. Such a morpheme which must be attached to another before it has meaning is called a *bound morpheme*, as opposed to a *free morpheme* such as *house*. In English, bound morphemes show great variation. The sound which indicates plurality in the words *houses*, *cats* (an *s* sound), *dogs* (a *z* sound), and *oxen* are quite different, and are known as allomorphs, having the same relationship to morphemes as do allophones to phonemes. Similar allomorphic variation is seen in the bound morpheme indicating negative qualities, as in the case of *ignoble*, *unsanitary*, *indistinct*, *immobile*, and *nonsense*. The sounds *ig*, *un*, *in*, and *non*, all convey the same meaning, and comprise the same morpheme.

Morphemes are combined in turn to form words, and although many words are single morphemes (*dog*, *float*) others contain many morphemes (*blackbird*, *unconstitutionality*). Length of a word is no indication of morpheme numbers; the word *Minnesota* in English is but a single morpheme, although its meaning is different in the Indian language from which it was taken, in which it has two morphemes (*Minne* and *Sota*). In some cases, a word is both morpheme and phoneme, as in the case of *I*, *a*, and *Oh* in English. Like phonemes, morphemes must be defined in terms of the language of which they are a part; the example of Minnesota is relevant in this case.

Using the concepts of phoneme and morpheme, structural linguists describe the structure of different languages, and define the rules for combining these units into larger constructs such as words and sentences. Each language has its own distinctive set of rules for phonemic and morphemic combination. In English, for example, the phoneme *ng*, which appears at the end of words like *sing* and *ring*, is never found at the beginning of a word, although it does occupy such a position in other languages. Similar rules govern the proper use of allomorphs. We do not say *cat-es* for *cats*, *unmodest* for *immodest*, or *nail-ed* for *nailed*. Such combinations *are* sometimes heard, from children who are only beginning to assimilate the rules for morphemic combination, and operate as much according to regularity as by cultural pattern; that is, they create words by analogy with others which they already know and use.

The structural units and rules which govern the form of a language have an interesting parallel in the structural rules which govern the form of material objects. In fact, words and artifacts have a lot more in common than it would seem at first glance. The same aspects which can be seen in artifacts are present in words. Consider for example the word *love*. Its functional aspect is that of describing a certain emotion in verb or noun form. Yet the context of the word has some effect on its specific function. Compare the function of this word in the sentence: "I just love that," when said with sarcasm and in the same sentence said with sincerity. The word *love* is made up of three phonemes; these are the structural analogues of the attributes of an artifact. This particular sound—*love*—is used by all English speakers for the same purposes, and it is a product of culturally patterned behavior just as a stone axe is.

This broad similarity between words and man-made objects is not particularly useful to the archaeologist faced with drawing inferences from his data. However, we may speculate a bit beyond this general level of correspondence and suggest some points of similarity which may ultimately have great significance to archaeological inference. Could it be that both words and artifacts are in fact different expressions of the same system? A little thought on the subject would make it appear to be so. We must emphasize that the discussion which follows is based on little more than conjecture in many ways, yet the close similarities which language and artifacts exhibit seem to indicate a vital and potentially exciting direction of archaeological analysis not yet fully realized.[19]

Words are products of human motor activity. They come into being through the action of muscles, directed by the mind through nerve impulses, on substance, in this case air. To produce the word *lock*, finite, measurable masses of air are shaped and given motion which results in sound. The size, form, and vibration frequency of the air masses which make up the word *lock* are measurable quantities. Words are transient things, to be sure, but at the time of their formation, they can be described in terms of sequences of formed air masses, combined to produce a culturally functional unit. The discrete segments of air in this case correspond to phonemes, so that three of these contribute to the configuration which constitutes the word *lock*. Alter the form of any of these units and the meaning of the word changes if this alteration is one which the culture using the word agrees to recognize as a level of significance sufficient to effect such a change.

Artifacts, like words, are the products of human motor activity, made through the action of muscles under mental guidance on the raw material involved. The resultant form of any artifact is a combination of structural units—attributes—which in any particular combination produce an object which has a specific function in the culture which made it. Change any one of these attributes and the functional significance will change if the change is sufficient to affect this significance. In other words, there may be structural units in artifacts which correspond to phonemes and morphemes in language, a correspondence which goes beyond simple analogy, reflecting an essential identity between language and objects in a structural sense. If this is true, in view of the close similarity between the way in which words and artifacts are created, might not words be but one aspect of a larger class of cultural products which includes all artifacts as well? If so, then the structural rules which linguists have formulated for language

[19] The following discussion is the result of long and stimulating conversations between the author and Professors Loring Brace of the University of California and Margaret Mead of the American Museum of Natural History.

might hold for the artifacts with which the archaeologist works. To check this interesting possibility, let us attempt to apply it to artifactual material.

In classifying the arrowheads from a site, we find three types. One type has a straight base and straight sides and notches near the base; another is similar but has an indented base, and the third has straight sides and base and lacks the notches (Fig. 14). This classification is based on three attri-

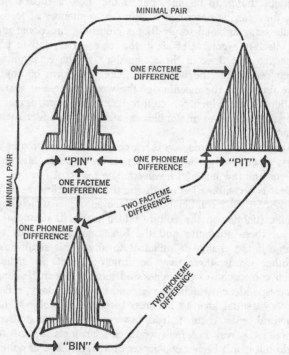

Fig. 14 Factemes and phonemes.

butes—side notching, basal notching, and the form of the sides. We must now make an assumption which cannot be determined from the data, but which will illustrate the relevance of structural linguistic units to artifacts. Assuming that notching the sides or notching the base had an effect on the functional significance of the arrowheads in the culture of their makers, arrowheads which are identical save for the presence or absence of the notches on the sides would form a minimal pair, distinguished on the basis of a single structural element (just as the words *hat* and *bat* form a minimal pair linguistically). In like manner, those arrowheads which are identical except for the presence or absence of notches in the base would also form a minimal pair if they served different purposes. Such notching is usually a factor of hafting—the way in which the arrowhead was attached to the arrowshaft—and thus such a functional difference is reasonable. Notching of the sides could then be seen as equivalent to the phoneme, and we might term such a unit a *facteme*.

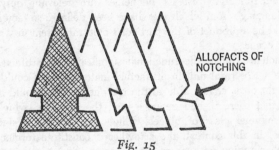

ALLOFACTS OF NOTCHING

Fig. 15

The definition of a facteme would then be the minimal class of attributes which affects the functional significance of the artifact. The notches might vary considerably in form, ranging from rather square to somewhat rounded, but as long as the functional significance of the arrowhead was not altered by this variation, such variants of this facteme would be regarded as allofacts (Fig. 15). There is an important parallel with language in this case. Allophonic variation derives in part from imperfections or variations in the speech-producing apparatus, and some variations in factemes are the result of imperfect expression of mental templates in the raw material, recalling some of the problems of template expression in subtractive technologies. Other allophonic variation stems from individual variation which is culture-free, and similar minor personal variations in factemes would constitute allofacts.

Such variation in the arrowheads as the form of the side which might be curved or straight without affecting their function could be a matter of personal whim. We have seen that function is more than a matter of technology, however, and if curved sides served to identify the arrowheads with a particular maker, this would constitute functional significance, and curved and straight sides would produce a minimal pair. The distinction between notched and unnotched sides in this system might not have prevailed in another culture. In such a case, notched and unnotched arrowheads might have been used for identical purposes, and the form of the side might have been the important determinant of technological function. Just as phonemes are relevant only to the language from which they have been defined, so factemes would be a product of the particular cultural system in which they occur.

Factemes affect the functional significance of artifacts. Is there a structural unit in artifactual material which could be thought of as comparable to the morpheme? We would suggest that there is, and define a unit, the *formeme*, which is the minimal class of objects which has functional significance. In this context, the arrowheads constitute formemes, which combine with other formemes to produce other artifacts. For example, an arrow could be seen as the combination of five formemes: shaft, stone head, feathers, cement used for attachment, and a painted design on the shaft. Each of these formemes can occur in other contexts. Similar points might be attached to short handles to serve as knives, similar shafts might be equipped with weights and used as spindles, and the feathers might be attached to quite different types of arrows or even to other objects, such as the "snow snakes" used by some American Indians in a game. The cement might be used in many other contexts, although its primary functional significance is that of joining material. The design, an ownership mark, could be used on other objects as well, and might be thought of as a bound formeme, since it could not occur alone (Fig. 16).

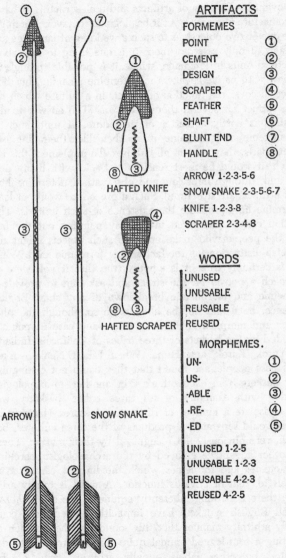

ARTIFACTS

FORMEMES

POINT	①
CEMENT	②
DESIGN	③
SCRAPER	④
FEATHER	⑤
SHAFT	⑥
BLUNT END	⑦
HANDLE	⑧

ARROW 1-2-3-5-6
SNOW SNAKE 2-3-5-6-7
KNIFE 1-2-3-8
SCRAPER 2-3-4-8

HAFTED KNIFE

HAFTED SCRAPER

WORDS

UNUSED
UNUSABLE
REUSABLE
REUSED

MORPHEMES.

UN-	①
US-	②
-ABLE	③
-RE-	④
-ED	⑤

UNUSED 1-2-5
UNUSABLE 1-2-3
REUSABLE 4-2-3
REUSED 4-2-5

ARROW

SNOW SNAKE

Fig. 16   Formemes and morphemes.

Obviously this view of artifacts and their structure is based on conjecture in a sense, yet it has logic in its favor. We might raise one or two objections to such a wedding of language and artifacts, if only as straw men. It is one thing to talk about structural units in language, where it is possible through interview with native speakers to determine meaning, but how do we discover the function of objects in a culture which has been extinct for several thousand years? The answer to this question is partly a matter of procedure. If units such as the facteme and formeme exist, then like their linguistic counterparts, they exist in all cultures. To implement this approach, it would be most sensible to begin with living peoples and, through interview and observation, determine how their artifacts are structured. Such a procedure would at least determine how probable the existence of such units is. This solution can be countered in part by pointing out the fact that the people who make and use such objects might not perceive distinctions on the factemic or formemic level. While this is certainly true, it is equally true that if you were to approach a person on the street and ask him to provide a phonemic and morphemic breakdown of any short English sentence, he would not be able to do so, though the phonemes and morphemes do exist. A striking case in point is provided by the baskets of three tribes of California Indians, the Yurok, Karok, and Hupa. When Lila O'Neale worked with these people, she found that they could not distinguish their baskets from each other's. Yet another anthropologist, working with examples of all three tribes' basketry was able to isolate a number of distinctive features (factemes?) which would separate the products of the three cultures, but which were obviously not recognized by their makers. There is another advantage enjoyed by the archaeologist searching for factemes and formemes which the linguist cannot avail himself to, that of obvious function. A word is totally arbitrary; there is nothing inherently equine in the sound *horse*, yet all English speakers have implicitly agreed in a completely arbitrary manner that this sound has the function of denoting a four-legged animal quite distinct from those designated by other labels equally arbitrary—cow, giraffe, okapi. Artifacts on the other hand often have a dimension of function inherent in their attributes; there is little doubt that an arrowhead was used for piercing, that a bowl was used as a container, or that an axe served to cut things down or up. Because of this advantage, at least a start can be made in determining the nature of factemic and formemic variation. Combine this advantage with a study of the artifacts of living peoples, and the chances of isolating units of the type defined here seem very good indeed.

Factemes and formemes, as we have defined them here, may or may not be the precise units which are combined according to the structural rules of a culture's artifacts, but most anthropologists do acknowledge the fact that some such structure exists, and that it is an important aspect of archaeological data. After all, if there were no structural rules, however broad, there would be no consistent patterning, and even the most arbitrary artifact type could not be defined and used to integrate assemblages.

Although the rules governing structure must be derived from the artifacts, they were originally the rules which dictated the form of the mental templates which produced the artifacts. Acknowledging this distinction is important to inference in archaeology.

Using a simple analogy with language, the formal analysis of artifacts and use of the types thus obtained for comparison is not too different from comparing languages only on the basis of form. We can inspect the vocabulary of two languages and determine with considerable assurance whether they are related by the degree to which they share vocabulary. However, if they also share in their grammatical rules, it is a virtual certainty that they are related. The reason for this is that it has been shown that vocabulary passes relatively easily from language to language; any high school student can recite a long list of borrowed words from other languages, including such exotic tongues as Eskimo (kayak) and Nahuatl (chocolate). Grammar, on the other hand, is singularly resistive to transfer from one language to another; we borrow extensively from the vocabularies of the Romance languages, but any similarities in grammar between English and French, for example, are the result of a remote common ancestry for both. In the same way, two assemblages might show a high degree of similarity in individual attributes, but only if they share similar rules for combining them can we infer that they are definitely related. This is not to say that there was not a connection of some kind between cultures sharing only in individual attributes, but the nature of the connection would differ greatly in each case.

Artifacts and their attributes do not move of their own volition, nor are they capable of biological breeding. If in our spatial and temporal ordering of a series of typed assemblages we detect similarities, it means that there was some movement of the templates which produced the objects, and templates are carried by people. By examining the nature of spatial and temporal distributions of artifacts in terms of their producing templates, we move closer to inference in terms of the people who carried the whole set of cultural ideas of which the templates were a part.

We can apply the concept of the mental template to show how archaeologists infer a number of quite specific cultural patterns in the past, including conquest, migration, trade, and certain marriage practices. In the spatial dimension, it is a common occurrence to find an area which produces a long series of virtually identical artifact types. These types are not only formally similar, but the mode of combining the attributes which constitute the types is equally similar. Such an area would seem to have been the location of an "idea pool," as indicated by a "template pool" which the archaeologist can see and measure. We discussed such a pattern in our consideration of space and time, and it was pointed out that there is a good chance that such a grouping would correspond to what would be seen as a culture by an anthropologist working with living people. However, closer inspection of the templates involved suggests that the degree of sharing and common occurrence is not entirely uniform. In fact, there is often a broad twofold division between those objects presumably made by males and those made by females. For example, baskets and milling equipment among the southern California Chumash of the early nineteenth century, and perhaps even earlier, is quite uniform over the entire area known to have been occupied by these people. Such uniformity contrasts sharply with the diversity seen in such artifacts as arrowheads, which differ considerably from site to site. The pattern is one of widespread rules for female manufactures, and isolated sets of somewhat different rules for male manufactures. Female templates are therefore widespread, male templates isolated. This can only mean that women were "widespread" and men "isolated." What cultural pattern is known to produce such an effect? Anthropologists concerned with the social structure and kinship organization of different peoples are interested in a set of customs known as postnuptial residence rules, or in simpler words, where people go to live after they are married. Several distinct rules have been defined, and they seem to correlate rather closely with other aspects of culture, such as economy, political organization, or complexity. For example, we Americans reside *neolocally*, apart from both parents. People who are *patrilocal* follow a custom whereby the woman lives with her husband's family after marriage; *matrilocality* is the mirror image, marked by residence of the married couple with the wife's family. We know that the Chumash followed a rule of patrilocal residence, combined with another practice, known as *local exogamy*. Exogamy simply means acquiring a mate from another group, and the group must be defined. In the Chumash case, this group is the local village. Thus, Chumash women would marry men from villages other than their own, moving there at marriage. The opposite of exogamy is *endogamy*, or marrying in, and the Chumash as a whole culture were largely endogamous because they usually married within their own tribe. They therefore practiced village exogamy and tribal endogamy.

Now a pattern of local exogamy combined with patrilocality would result in male templates and their structural rules being retained in the village, so that in time they would become somewhat different through the effects of isolation. Females, moving from village to village at marriage, would be responsible for the circulation of templates and rules over the entire Chumash area and a little beyond. Such a pattern is that which we have observed, and it permits the tentative inference of a social practice solely from a consideration of the structural aspects of the artifacts. In the case of the arrowheads, although all villages produced broadly similar types, these differ greatly in relative frequency from site to site. Thus simple formal analysis would indicate some connection, but until the dynamics of template dispersal and occurrence were considered, we could not arrive at a statement of the social practice which caused it.[20]

Diffusion

The subject of diffusion is one of considerable anthropological and archaeological interest. Diffusion is the spread of cultural ideas, and a number of things can bring it about. If we find similar artifacts and house types in sites which are so far apart that they probably do not belong to the same culture, we can either attribute the similarity to the independent invention of very similar traits at each location or suggest that they spread from one point to another. Unless the similarities are extremely vague and tenuous, the latter explanation is demanded.

Archaeologists frequently recognize two types of diffusion, *primary* and *secondary*. We have seen how space-time slopes can indicate the direction and rate of diffusion, but this method does not tell us whether the diffusion was primary or secondary. Primary diffusion is accompanied by the movement of large numbers of people, either through migration or military conquest. Secondary diffusion on the other hand involves the spread of ideas from village to village, or culture to culture, with no accompanying population movements on any large scale. We can imagine the kind of movement which would produce secondary diffusion; exogamy between cultures in both directions which would cause the spread of ideas, simple visiting between communities and learning about new and attractive things, and perhaps even trade of objects which would act as inspirations for innovation in their new cultural context.

With the nature of template movement in mind, it is obvious that primary and secondary diffusion would produce quite different patterns of attribute sharing. Two cultural fac-

[20] For a good discussion of the social practices which lead to such patterns in archaeological materials, see R. C. Owen, "The Patrilocal Band: A Linguistically and Culturally Hybrid Social Unit," *American Anthropologist*, Vol. 67, No. 3, 1965.

tors which might produce primary diffusion are migration and conquest. In the case of migration, we would expect to see complete templates connected with both sexes present in both the culture of origin and the culture which presumably was the end result of the migration. One of the most dramatic cases of such large-scale transfer of templates is to be seen at the Point of Pines Ruin in southern Arizona.[21] This ruin is a pueblo of some 300 rooms built between A.D. 1200 and 1400. Within this complex there is a series of seventy or more rooms which are markedly different from the others in the pueblo. They are larger, and lack the stone-lined fire pits, storage cubicles, and meal-grinding bins typical of all other rooms in the complex. Archaeologists excavated twenty-one of these distinctive rooms, and found that all but three had been burned, in marked contrast to all other rooms in the pueblo, only one of which had been destroyed by fire. The pottery in the burned rooms, although locally manufactured, as indicated by the type of clay used, was typical in its form of the pottery of the Hopi-Kayenta area 200 miles to the north. A few of the pots were actually from the northern area, having been made there, and a few were of local manufacture and form. Near the burned out rooms a D-shaped *kiva*—an underground ceremonial chamber—was found. This kiva was totally different from the other fifteen kivas excavated at Point of Pines. D-shaped kivas are also typical of the Hopi-Kayenta region. Fragments of burned wooden implements from the rooms exhibited tree ring growth patterns which were more similar in detail to the patterns from the north than that of the Point of Pines region. Many of the burned rooms contained large quantities of charred corn. This corn was different from that grown locally at the time of occupation, but similar on the other hand to that of the area to the north.

We see in this example the wholesale transfer of templates and patterns typical of another area, and the same configuration can be identified in the area from which it presumably came. Such a complete re-creation of an entire assemblage in another location almost demands identification as the end

21 R. H. Thompson (ed.), *Migrations in New World Culture History* (Tucson: University of Arizona Press, 1958).

product of a true migratory movement of a fairly large population, large enough to maintain its identity in the new location. In that portion of the ruin at Point of Pines which was occupied immediately following the burning of the intrusive complex, few of these distinctive alien traits continue, although even later, corn of the type found in the rooms makes its appearance in some quantity. It is noteworthy that this interpretation of the evidence is made even more probable by the extremely precise chronological control afforded by the use of dendrochronological dates. Dendrochronological evidence even adds further explanation to an already clear picture; the source area to the north was undergoing a period of drought at the time of the postulated migration, which perhaps made it necessary for the people to move south at that time.

If considerable amalgamation between migrating culture and the indigenous culture in the area into which the migration occurred were to take place, one might expect a combination of elements from both cultures, but at the level of whole templates rather than individual attributes at first. Such attribute mixing might eventually occur, through the mutual influence of the templates of each culture, but the initial mixing should be of complete templates only. We can see such a process rather clearly in the Great Plains, where the village layouts of two cultures combined in such a way that the source of each feature is obvious. In A.D. 1500, the Indians of the Missouri river valley in South Dakota lived in communities of long rectangular houses, often surrounded by rectangular fortification systems of bastioned palisades and moats. To the south in Nebraska, circular houses were the rule, and bastioned fortifications were lacking. Early in the sixteenth century, droughts drove the occupants of the circular house villages north into the area occupied by the rectangular house villages. The site which shows the result of the amalgamation of these two distinct types of villages has circular houses similar to those in Nebraska surrounded by a bastioned fortification system typical of the indigenous population of the region. The pottery from these houses also shows some aspects of admixture, although in many cases, it is at the attribute level only, suggesting that some time had passed since the initial contact, resulting in the incorporation of attributes from both ceramic systems into new template combinations.

Secondary diffusion does not involve the movement of large populations or even of people except on a limited "Brownian Movement" basis. Under such circumstances, we would expect a more random mixing of attributes, with little or no complete template recurrence at distant points from the source of ideas. This is the type of diffusion indicated by the majority of archaeological assemblages which share similarities over great distances. For example, the pottery of the prehistoric Hohokam culture of southern Arizona is characterized by red on buff painting, a style which extends far to the south into Mexico. Yet the designs painted in these colors do not show close similarities to those to the south, and we can best account for this sharing by suggesting that it came from a secondary diffusion process. In a similar manner, the baskets made by the Gabrieleno Indians, who lived just to the south of the Chumash, but spoke an entirely different language, share with the Chumash the use of raw materials and the use of a band of decoration encircling the area just inside the rim. Yet the placement of this band is somewhat different from that used by the Chumash, and the form and location of designs within the body of the basket, while reminiscent of the treatment given such elements by the Chumash, is nonetheless distinctive, so that in considering the rules of attribute combination, one would hardly conclude that the Chumash and Gabrieleno shared in the templates of basket design. In this case, exogamy and intermarriage between the groups along the zone of contact between them could account for the similarities observed—another mode of secondary diffusion.

The exchange of objects through trade between communities or cultures is also responsible for widespread similarities in artifacts. If an artifact received in trade by a people inspires copying, the result is a local reproduction of a major template pattern. However, in many cases, since the object being copied exists in its new context in the absence of the template and its structural rules, there is a measure of irrationality in the reproduction. Obvious cases of this type of copying include polished-stone copies of metal axes received in trade in Northern Europe several thousand years before Christ. The metal prototypes, received in trade by people who did not possess a technology of metal casting, were copied in stone in all their attributes, including the seam in the metal which resulted from the two piece mold used in their manufacture. Similar clay copies of metal tools from ancient Mesopotamia also show the casting seams reproduced in this manner. Although such illogical copying is usually not as obvious as these two cases might indicate, the reproduction of artifacts by people not aware of the structural aspect of those artifacts will not be governed by the rules which produced them in the culture where they were made. In some cases, this difference will be sufficiently obvious to permit the inference of trade as an explanation of the primary factor involved in a secondary diffusion process. In other cases, technical analysis of the clays of pottery, of the metals used in cups or spearheads, or of the stone used to manufacture axes will tell the archaeologist that the distribution of certain types of artifacts is the result of trade over a wide area. Even nonartifactual materials often indicate trade, as shown by the presence of Pacific shells in sites far inland in Arizona, or obsidian from the Rocky Mountains turning up in sites in Ohio.

Before leaving the subject of diffusion, we must realize that the cultural practices which cause similar objects to be found over large areas were probably diverse, and while exogamy, migration, trade, or conquest can be seen as possible causal agents for such distributions, others less obvious or more unusual might have been responsible. We must operate according to probabilities in all archaeological inference, but at the same time we must remember that we can never be one hundred percent certain that our explanation is the correct one. A striking example of a practice which leads to wide spatial distributions of artifacts is provided by Heider's study of the Dugum Dani of the highlands of New Guinea.[22] These people are quite warlike, and Dani villages are forever in-

---

[22] K. G. Heider, *The Dugum Dani. A Papuan Culture in the West New Guinea Highlands* (unpublished Ph.D. dissertation, Harvard University, 1965).

olved in chronic warfare with their neighbors on all sides.
A quotation from Heider's study will highlight the causes of
arrow distributions throughout the Dani area; a process
which could have prevailed in the past time and time again.

Arrows are shot back and forth on the battlefield. The archers arrive at the battle with a dozen or so arrows, and at the end of the
day leave with about the same number, but all are different from
those he brought. Arrows shot by the enemy are followed in their
flight, snatched up, and quickly shot back into the enemy ranks. I
watched one arrow make four such trips until it was finally retired
from the battle in the body of an archer.

There is no special significance attached to an enemy arrow
which hits the ground. It may be shot back, or eventually carried
off the field, to be used in a different battle. However, an arrow
which causes a wound is carefully saved by the victim, and placed
in the rafters of the men's house, in front of the fireplace. If the
arrow is unable to be removed, and eventually results in death, it is
removed from the corpse before cremation. (354)

The variation in design of fighting arrows in terms of patterns of
barbs, and notches, and decoration of tip and shaft, is particularly
striking. There is tremendous within-group variation, but remarkably little between-group variation—the group here being the arrows
carried by any one man. Although a man usually carries a dozen
or so arrows, rarely does he carry two similar arrows. The exceptions occur when a man has just made a set of arrows. But after
the first battle, these have been shot out over the battlefield, picked
up by various individuals, and carried to different villages. (362)

Arrows are the one item more rapidly diffused because of warfare. Men come together from kilometers apart to fight against each
other, and incidentally exchange arrows, on a common front. Then,
the next week, each may be fighting and exchanging arrows on
still other fronts, more kilometers apart. There is, to be sure, peace-
ful trading in arrows; but the constant state of war throughout
the Dani area assures that arrows will be in constant movement
from one region to another. (363–64)

No further comment is necessary.

Chapter VIII

BEHAVIOR

The various methods and techniques of archaeology, from radiocarbon dating to grid layouts, from typology to template analysis, are all directed in some way toward the explanation of behavior in the past. We have said that archaeology tries to describe culture history before writing—prehistory—and to reconstruct extinct cultural systems that existed at different times and in different locations. Both objectives of archaeology involve the reconstruction of past behavioral patterns. After all, what is culture if not that patterned behavior characteristic of the human animal?

Although prehistory and archaeology are frequently considered to be synonymous, prehistory is actually only one segment of archaeology. The other segment lacks a convenient label; it might be called paleoethnography, paleoethnology, or both. Ethnography and ethnology are both aspects of cultural anthropology, the study of living peoples in cultural terms. Ethnography entails the descriptive study of individual cultures, while ethnology is the cross-cultural comparative analysis of ethnographic data with the hope of making some kind of theoretical statements concerning culture in general. While the term paleoanthropology has recently become current, it involves both the historical and ethnological aspects of prehistoric cultures as well as certain biological aspects. Paleoethnography and paleoethnology, on the other hand, would be primarily restricted to the cultural dimension of man. It may actually be redundant to use the prefix *paleo-* in this case, since they involve aims identical to those of ethnography and ethnology. The differences lie in the particular analytical methods employed, and are due to the differences in the types of data involved, but the results which are obtained are quite similar.

The behavioral aspect of archaeological data is concerned with the way in which man's behavior is reflected in the objects he makes. We have seen some examples of such behavioral reflections in our consideration of other inferential

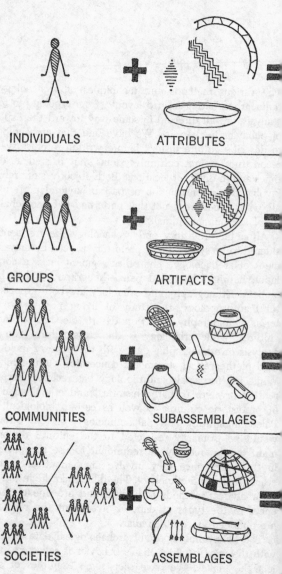

INDIVIDUALS + ATTRIBUTES =

GROUPS + ARTIFACTS =

COMMUNITIES + SUBASSEMBLAGES =

SOCIETIES + ASSEMBLAGES =

Fig. 17 Behavioral

ATTRIBUTE PATTERNING
REFLECTS INDIVIDUAL
BEHAVIOR PATTERNS

ARTIFACTS

ARTIFACT PATTERNING
REFLECTS GROUP
BEHAVIOR PATTERNS

SUBASSEMBLAGES

SUBASSEMBLAGE
PATTERNING REFLECTS
COMMUNITY
BEHAVIOR PATTERNS

ASSEMBLAGES

ASSEMBLAGE
PATTERNING REFLECTS
SOCIETAL
BEHAVIOR PATTERNS

ARCHAEOLOGICAL CULTURES

evels and patterning.

aspects of archaeology. We now place the stress on the nature of the articulation between the patterning observed in archaeological materials and the patterning of the culture of their makers.

Levels of behavior

Human cultural behavior occurs on four levels. The individual has certain ways of doing things and of thinking about things which he shares with no other person, living or dead. In these habits he is unique. Such idiosyncratic behavior may really not be cultural if it is not passed on to other individuals, but behavior shared by several individuals certainly is. Other patterns of behavior are shared by the individual with a number of people who form some kind of an interacting group—a family, a club, or those members of his community who are of the same sex. Most communities will have a number of such groups, and an individual may belong to several. There are other patterns of behavior which the individual shares with all other members of his community. Finally, there are behavioral patterns which are universal to the total culture of which an individual is a member. Thus in observing the behavior of a single person, we see that some of his actions and beliefs are his alone, some he shares only with the members of his family or a similar minimal group of people, others are shared with all the people in his community, and a few are shared by every member of his culture.

It would be reasonable to expect to find these four levels of patterning in artifactual materials, since such materials reflect the behavior of the culture which produced them. We can distinguish certain modules which are combined in a patterned way to build up assemblages (Fig. 17). The basic module is the attribute. Attributes are combined to form artifacts by individuals; while these vary somewhat in their precise form, there are certain basic classes, factemes perhaps, which constitute meaningful units of patterning. Thus the patterning of attributes reflects patterning in the behavior of individuals. The artifacts which result from such patterned sets of attributes are second level modules. Artifacts are combined to form subassemblages which are given pattern by various minimal groups within a community. For example, eed beaters, carrying baskets, grinding stones, parching trays, and leaching baskets constitute a subassemblage within a typical California Indian assemblage, patterned in its repeated combination by the females of the community. Bows, arrows, scrapers, and knives constitute a male-associated subassemblage within the same total assemblage. If subassemblages are patterned in their combination of certain artifacts by groups within the community, then assemblages reflect in their patterning the shared activity of a community as a whole, with the subassemblages constituting the modules in this case. Finally, the patterning manifested by whole assemblage modules reflects behavior characteristic of entire cultures. It must be emphasized that when we talk about patterning, we mean that which is seen in two or more artifacts, subassemblages, or assemblages, since patterning quite obviously cannot be described unless it can be shown to be repetitive.

The significance of each of these levels of patterning to inference from the behavioral aspect will become clear through a number of specific examples. Some of these examples permit checking for accuracy by considering the known historical and ethnological circumstances which prevailed at the time; others lack this control, and show how the behavioral aspect of inference can be used in truly prehistoric situations. The same problems of precision of inference which were made explicit by the Dani arrow case prevail in behavioral inference, as indeed they do in all inferential procedures. However, the cases which are described below indicate the direction and potential of behavioral inference.

Artifacts and individuals

Recent studies of the manner in which attributes are combined to create artifacts promise to provide insights regarding certain features of social organization in the past. One such investigation involves an examination of the manner in which the attributes of pottery design were combined through time as this might reflect changes in the patterned behavior of the potters.[23] The potters in this case were the Arikara Indians

[23] James J. F. Deetz, *The Dynamics of Stylistic Change in Arikara Ceramics* (Urbana: University of Illinois Press, 1965).

of the Missouri river valley, whom we met earlier, as they changed their pottery types while en route upstream.

In 1958, a clearly stratified three component Arikara site was excavated by the author in central South Dakota. The components represent these people as they were between 1700 and 1780. The pottery from the site could be clearly sorted according to component. When the assemblage was taken to the laboratory for analysis, it was discovered that the pottery from the earliest component could be placed into clearly defined typological groups, but the pottery from the latest component practically defied classification according to the same attributes used in the earlier successful sorting. The intermediate component was intermediate also in terms of typological clarity.

We decided to investigate this pattern further, and in order to be more precise and comprehensive, we prepared a very detailed list of over one hundred attributes for the collection. These attributes formed the basis of a code which was used to describe each potsherd on an IBM card, and the completed set of cards was submitted to a computer which told us the degree of association between every pair of attributes in the sample from each component. This operation, which involved hundreds of thousands of individual computations, showed that the difficulty in creating typological categories in the later two component samples stemmed from a progressive lowering of the degree of association between the attributes in the samples. In the earliest component, there was a tendency for attributes to form rather tight clusters, which were reflected in type categories. If a given attribute was found to be associated with certain attributes, it would not be found as often with certain others. In the later two components these attribute clusters tended to become much looser. By the time of the latest component, there was almost random association between attributes, so that each attribute occurred just about as often with every other one, making the establishment of type categories almost impossible. In terms of the templates which led to the production of the pottery, and the rules for their formation, we can see that earlier in time there were a number of somewhat different idea sets, which tended to become less distinct and to blend more with each other with the passage of time.

What possible explanations could be found for this change in patterning? We have said that individuals are responsible for the combination of attributes into patterned sets. In these terms, there would seem to have been some factor in the earliest component which caused numbers of individuals to behave in much the same way in the manufacture of pottery, and this factor apparently became less significant with the passage of time. We investigated Arikara ethnography and culture history to seek an explanation for this change.

The Arikara began their slow movement up the Missouri River sometime later in the sixteenth century. They were originally a part of the Pawnee Indians, who resided in northeastern Nebraska. The Pawnee and earlier Arikara were organized in large families based on matrilocal residence: grandmothers, mothers, and daughters lived together in large earth-covered lodges, where they were joined at marriage by their husbands, who had grown up in other households. We know from ethnological theory that such households frequently develop in situations where women produce the majority of the food and in which there is a large degree of permanence in the location of the communities. Such were the circumstances in earlier times among the Pawnee and Arikara, but moving north into the drainage of the Missouri River, the Arikara underwent a number of changes in the structure of their society, ultimately leading to a breakdown in the former strict rule of matrilocality. These changes were brought on by a different set of adaptive problems presented to Arikara culture by the new environment. The Missouri River in South Dakota was not as well supplied with trees as were the timber-streaked prairies of Nebraska. The Arikara were forced to move their villages as often as every five to ten years simply because they had exhausted the available timber supply in the vicinity.

As they moved through the new area, the Arikara became involved with two cultures which demanded further adjustments and modifications of their society. The first of these new peoples were the Dakota Indians, who during the eighteenth century had acquired horses and guns from encroaching Europeans. These new commodities were obtained through trade—horses from the south in exchange for guns from the north, and the Arikara found themselves as middlemen in this trade exchange. It was not uncommon for a band of Arikara men to travel west to the Black Hills with guns and food, trade these items for horses which they would then take into the eastern Dakotas to exchange for more guns to trade to the south and west. While they gained certain wealth from this exchange, the Arikara also became involved in sporadic warfare with the Dakota, and late in the eighteenth century, they lost control of their position as go-betweens.

The second group of people with whom the Arikara became involved were the Europeans, who exerted pressures on them as well as on their Dakota neighbors, leading further to the breakdown of their culture. European contact led to their depopulation also, since epidemics of smallpox, a European disease, swept the Arikara, reducing their numbers drastically.

The most severe pressures were placed on the Arikara during the eighteenth century, the time represented by our site. Almost every change effected by these pressures affected the nature of the basic Arikara residence group. The earlier large matrilocal groups were broken up, and women became more mobile within the community, often residing with other families than their own. The reduction in the size of the household can also be seen in the progressive reduction in house size in Arikara sites of the eighteenth century. Between 1700 and 1800, Arikara houses changed their diameters from fifty to twenty-five feet, a fourfold reduction in living space.

We were confronted with two pictures of change, one archaeological, the other ethnographic, but occurring among the same people at the same time. How were these patterns related? It was most logical and efficient to explain the blurring and blending of attributes through time as reflecting the change in the channeling of behavioral patterns related to pottery manufacture. Earlier in time, women who resided together, and who were related, would share in idea sets related to pottery which were more or less different from those held by other similar residential groups. As long as isolation and regular transmission of pottery making behavioral patterns were preserved by the large matrilocal families, a number of somewhat different kinds of pottery would be made within a village. But when these groups were broken up, a more random mixing of ideas, and their constituent attributes, would occur. This was precisely the pattern of change which we observed in the pottery, occurring concurrently with the disappearance of matrilocal families. Since Arikara women made the pottery, and grandmothers often instructed granddaughters in the art of pottery manufacture, the breakdown of the large families would remove the daughters from the influence of grandmother instruction, as well as dissolve work groups of related women.

Another example of this type of behavioral inference comes from a prehistoric context in the American Southwest.[24] The archaeologist who conducted this study, William Longacre, excavated a thirty-nine-room pueblo which was occupied between A.D. 1100 and 1250. Two kivas were associated with the pueblo, one associated with the rooms at the northern end of the pueblo, the other with the rooms at the southern end. Analysis of the attributes of the pottery from northern and southern room and kiva groups, done with the aid of a computer, showed that each group was characterized by a somewhat different set of designs, forming distinctive clusters associated with dwelling areas and kivas. Burials in the adjacent areas occurred in two groups which produced pottery similar to that from each room and kiva group in each case. On the basis of this evidence, Longacre postulates two localized family groups each organized according to a rule of matrilocal residence.

These examples of the reflection of behavioral patterns, and their changes, in the patterning of the attributes combined by the individual, are reminiscent of the example already described for the Chumash in their manufacture of baskets and arrowheads. In both cases, we see the behavioral mode of the individual being a function of the mode of transmission of mental templates, an aspect of culturally determined behavior which can be inferred with high probability from the

[24] William A. Longacre, "Archaeology as Anthropology: A Case Study," *Science*, Vol. 144, 1964.

objects which are the products of these patterns of behavior.

Attribute patterning can reflect behavioral patterning of other kinds apart from those which are the result of changes in social organization. In examining certain attribute patterns, we can make statements about changes in such cultural realms as technology. An interesting demonstration of partial technological change under culture contact, characterized by a blending of the old and new ways of doing a task, is shown by certain artifacts from a Fransciscan mission in southern California.

When the Franciscans founded the missions of California, they introduced a number of new technologies to the Indians whom they were converting to Christianity. Indian men were put to work in a broad variety of crafts which they had never known before. At La Purisima Mission, near Lompoc, California, a tanning vat was excavated which had been used for soaking hides in lime and then in a tanbark oak solution. Two vats were used for this purpose, one for lime and one for the tanning process itself. When these vats were excavated, a number of distinctive bone tools was found on their floors. These were beamers, used to remove hair from the lime-soaked hides prior to putting them into the tanning solution. Now the form of these beamers is quite similar to bone beamers and scrapers found in aboriginal sites in the vicinity. Thus most of the attributes which contribute to their form are native in origin. However, the material used to make the beamers was ribs from cattle. Cattle, of course, were a European introduction. Although other bone may have been available, and metal knives certainly were, the Indians apparently preferred to use the bone of an introduced animal to fashion an implement which was formally similar to those which they had known before, to accomplish a phase of a technology which they had acquired from the Franciscans. The significance of this pattern to understanding process is that there was not a complete replacement of aboriginal attributes by introduced ones; instead, a blend of introduced materials and technology with an aboriginal function and form resulted.

The adaptation of introduced attributes to a set of indigenous structural rules is also seen in two remarkable baskets made by two Chumash neophytes at Ventura Mission (Fig.

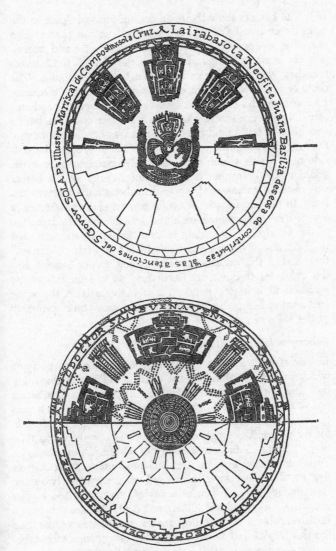

Fig. 18 Chumash presentation baskets.

18). The baskets show the royal coat of arms of Spain in the main decorative field, and are inscribed with a presentation statement in Spanish. Although both coat of arms and inscription are attributes totally foreign to the aboriginal Chumash set, they were incorporated into the basket decoration. The coats of arms were modified into radial decorative elements. In one case, the inscription replaced the principal band surrounding the rim of the basket; in the other case, the basket was given a traditional band, the rim was finished in normal fashion, and the inscription was then added around the outside of a basket which was essentially complete prior to its addition. In the former case, the center design of the basket was radially symmetrical, as are all aboriginal Chumash designs. In the latter case, the center is most uncharacteristically asymmetrical; combined with the less integrated adaptation of the inscription by adding it atop the design suggests that the behavior of the maker of this basket was less "Chumash" than that of the woman who maintained proper balance and the old rules throughout. Here then we see an interesting variation in behavior between two individuals in the same community, doing the same task at the same time, probably at the same request.

Subassemblages and interacting groups

Just as attributes are combined by individuals into patterns which permit the archaeologist to make inferences regarding the behavioral patterning of those individuals, so artifacts are at times combined into groups which reflect in their patterning the behavior of the groups of individuals responsible for their form. Once again we can see an example of this type of patterning in the archaeology of California missions. La Purisima Mission had, in 1814, a large Indian barracks, over five hundred feet long, composed of contiguous two-room "apartment" units. When a series of these apartments was excavated, a significant difference could be seen between Indian artifacts representing males and those representing females. Males and females comprise two groups whose behavior is reflected in artifact groupings. We can speak of male subassemblages and female subassemblages. It is known historically that with the exception of unmarried young girls, the barracks housed complete family groups—mother, father, and children. Yet those artifacts representing aboriginal Indian culture, and similar to those found on contemporary aboriginal sites, were almost totally lacking in male-associated objects. Even waste materials, such as stone flakes, which might have resulted from the manufacture of arrowheads and stone knives, were absent. On the other hand, female-associated artifacts—baskets, seed-grinding equipment, stone-baking slabs—were as common as they are in non-mission Indian sites. We might infer from this peculiar difference that behavior which would lead to the groupings of artifacts similar to those of pre-mission time was quite different. In this case, we have an historical record to check our inference, and it tells us that such a conclusion is correct. Under missionization, men's roles were profoundly changed, from hunting to ranching, farming, and craft activities, while female roles continued almost unchanged, still being directed at food preparation, and the manufacture of artifact groups which served this purpose. Thus the differences in subassemblage configurations in the mission on the one hand and in the outlying villages on the other reflect differences in behavior on the part of males and females in each cultural context.

Another example of the patterning in artifact groups as it reflects minimal group behavior, this time family groups, comes from our knowledge of Colonial cemeteries in New England. Gravestones are artifacts just as much as pottery, baskets, or stone tools, and in this case, a change in behavior on the part of individual families is seen in the changes which take place in gravestone groupings. Until about 1790, all families of Puritan New England who were faithful church members buried their dead in the churchyard. While one can see family areas within cemeteries beside the churches, such groupings are secondary to the larger aggregation of burials which represent the parish, a larger group within the total community and culture. However, due to the slow trend to secularization of the practice of burial, and in part due to a growing concern about burial within towns as a threat to sanitation, there was a breakdown in church control of the placement of the dead. Such placement is, of course, reflected by the placement of gravestones, the artifacts in this case. At the close of the eighteenth century, we see for the first time small groups of gravestones, representing single families, completely separated from the churchyard groups. By 1800, a number of small family plots had made their appearance in the area where formerly all burial had been in the churchyard. Behavioral change in this case reflects defection from the strong central control of the church, and family units become autonomous in terms of disposal of the dead, and more influential than the church in determining this aspect of behavior.

Yet another example of this type of patterning, and the type of inference which it permits, comes from a culture known as the Mousterian, which was present in Europe and the Near East 45,000 or more years ago. The Mousterian people, known as the Neanderthals, were hunters, living from the herds of large game animals available at the time. Analysis of Mousterian assemblages in terms of tool groupings suggests that there are a number of subassemblages which reflect specific activities of certain segments of the population.[25] For example, at small sites which are distinct from large sites thought to represent major communities, one repeatedly encounters groupings of tools clearly connected with hunting and butchering—spear points, stone knives and scrapers, tools for cutting bone. Such sites were probably hunting camps. Another subassemblage has the contextual aspect of occurrence with fire areas and the tools in this set suggest the manufacture of other tools—a domestic tool-making subassemblage. These groupings then permit the inference of hunting groups distinct from domestic groups, and these in turn distinct from others yet different, and indicated by other consistently recurring tool sets. Any one of the tools of one subassemblage is usually accompanied by the others of the same group; in this way, we see groupings of tools, rather distinctive in their form of combination, reflecting the behavior of sections of the community just as groupings of attributes in earlier Arikara pottery reflected the behavior of a number of

[25] L. R. and S. R. Binford, "A Preliminary Analysis of Functional Variability in the Mousterian of Levallois Facies," *Paleoanthropology* (special volume of *American Anthropologist,* 1966).

individuals within a single household. Although the modules of patterning differ in each case—attributes with individuals; tools with groups—the manner in which behavioral patterning is reflected in modular patterning is identical.

Assemblages and communities

Behavior on the part of a complete community, as far as it can be seen to have a pattern from observing a number of cases, is reflected in the patterning seen in complete assemblages. In our discussion of function, we saw how a whole assemblage served a unified function to the community employing it. In a more specific way, behavior universal to an entire community is frequently reflected in a particular type of feature, the remains of structures. The archaeological study of community and settlement pattern is an important one, and a considerable quantity of study of this aspect of archaeological data has been done. A good example of how behavior on the part of a community is reflected in the patterning of the structures within a site is provided by changes in Arikara community plan. Prior to the pressures exerted on the Arikara by Europeans and Dakota, their communities were arranged in rather loose sets of houses, lacking in fortification. Large underground, bell-shaped storage pits were frequently placed adjacent to the houses, but outside. When the need for defense against enemies presented itself, the behavior of the community related to the arrangement of houses changed to a pattern placing emphasis on defense. The result was a different layout of houses and storage pits. This new pattern was that of tightly spaced houses, enclosed by a circular palisade and moat. Since the space between the houses was reduced by this practice, it was more practical to place the storage pits within the houses, in their floors. Sites which are fortified and late in the Arikara area usually have large numbers of storage pits in their floors. For this reason, the progressive reduction in the size of Arikara houses which occurred during the eighteenth century is reversed during the period of fortification, and this enlargement probably came about since more floor space was needed to gain an equal amount of living room while moving the storage facilities indoors.

Note that the modules in this case are houses; with their artifactual contents, houses can be thought of as subassemblages reflecting the behavior of households, minimal community groups. Thus community behavior is reflected in the manner in which the community structures those subassemblages which represent family groups within the community.

Patterning exhibited by a number of assemblages would be expected to reflect the patterning of behavior on the part of the society as a whole. Thus comparisons of the manner in which assemblages are grouped into larger units are also potentially comparisons of behavior common to different societies. Studies of settlement pattern provide examples of this type of patterning. Settlement pattern is sometimes thought of as distinct from community pattern, and the term used to denote the way in which a certain society arranges its communities on the landscape. For example, the settlement pattern typical of the Mayan civilization of pre-Columbian Guatemala and Mexico is characterized by ceremonial centers—groups of pyramids, temples and plazas, scattered through the jungle, with a fairly even distribution of the population, as reflected by house remains, between the ceremonial complexes. This pattern of arrangement of houses and temples is distinctive of Maya culture and society as a whole. It is in sharp contrast to the pattern seen in the Valley of Mexico, where the Teotihuacán civilization of the early centuries of the Christian era placed emphasis on urban concentration. In this case, the ceremonial center is a nucleus of a tightly grouped urban complex, a true city, unlike the widely spread settlement pattern of the Maya during the same time.

The examples of each of the four levels of patterning given above are just that—examples—and were chosen because they are particularly explicit. However, we must remember that even at the individual level certain attributes are universal to an entire society, as are certain aspects of subassemblage patterns and assemblages. In the same way, certain behavioral patterns are shared by the individual with all other members of his culture. Yet there is great value in considering the nature of patterning and variation at the lower, more specific levels, since in this way, we ultimately reach an understanding of the behavior of the individual and his immediate social group within the total culture. The attributes used by the Arikara women in pottery manufacture were certainly partly those of all Arikara women, and other households, in other communities, may have produced very similar patterns. But it was still possible to make a reasonable and probable inferential statement regarding the behavior of these individual women, and how it changed through time, by considering the patterning seen in attributes at a specific site.

Developmental stages

There is yet one other concept of modern archaeology which we have not considered, that of the *developmental stage*. The stage concept is employed primarily in prehistory as a means of rather arbitrarily dividing world culture history into a number of levels, identified by certain cultural criteria. In a sense, the developmental stage constitutes a fifth level of cultural behavioral patterning that is shared by a number of societies, but since it is somewhat more arbitrary than those modules discussed earlier, it is better to consider it separately.

Archaeologists have divided the prehistory of man into a set of five distinct stages of development in both the Old and the New World. New World stages are approximately the same as those of the Old World though occurring generally later.

In the Old World, it is customary to distinguish *Paleolithic, Mesolithic, Neolithic, Bronze Age,* and *Iron Age* stages of development. In the New World, approximately equivalent stages are termed *Lithic, Archaic, Formative, Classic,* and *Post-Classic.* In neither case is there anything "natural" about the fivefold division; the stages are somewhat arbitrary, but defined by a set of criteria which are applicable in all cases. In classifying archaeological data in developmental stages, the archaeologist is in fact grouping numbers of prehistoric societies into classes based on a number of shared features. In this sense, the stage does have a behavioral aspect, but in a very broad sense.

The Paleolithic stage in the Old World represents over ninety-five percent of man's existence on earth, from nearly two million years ago until ca. 10,000 B.C. During the entire time occupied by the Paleolithic stage, a geological event known as the Pleistocene, or Ice Age, occurred. Four separate glaciations took place, characterized by the accumulation of ice in polar zones, and the southward advance of this ice into more temperate regions. The beginning of the Pleistocene is marked by a number of changes including the appearance of a new group of animals, which include in their numbers man himself. Man developed from a form hardly human in appearance to his present physical form during the Pleistocene, and since the Pleistocene and the Paleolithic are roughly contemporary, beginning and ending at the same time, we can say that man evolved to modern form during the Paleolithic. But Paleolithic is a term used to designate a cultural developmental stage. Its etymology gives some indication of what it involves—the Old Stone Age. It was during the Paleolithic that man made his most basic inventions, and gave initial form to his culture. Language, human social organization, fire, shelter, clothing, weapons, and religion, all had their beginnings during the Paleolithic. We do not even know just where or when each of these important innovations took place, but they are all clearly present at the end of the Paleolithic, and were not at the beginning. Man was a hunter during the entire Paleolithic. Archaeological evidence from this stage is somewhat limited, with few exceptions being tools of stone, antler, and bone, and shelters and the remains of structures from near the end. We see in the stone tools left by Paleolithic man the painfully slow but quickening development of his technology. The earliest tools are simple, sharpened river cobbles known as choppers. Over hundreds of thousands of years, these become refined. First, we see the development of fully flaked stone implements known as hand axes, although it is not certain that they served such a purpose. These are supplemented by tools made from stone flakes, and heavy stone cleavers probably used for dismembering the carcasses of large animals. It is somewhat easier to ascribe a specific function to these later tools. The earliest "choppers" probably served a multitude of purposes, but we can be certain of few if any of them specifically.

The slow development of a few basic multipurpose tools continues from over a million years ago until about 45,000 B.C. Then, we see a dramatic quickening in the pace of development. This spurt in development seems in some way to be a function of man's first invasion of colder climates. Earlier, the evidence suggests that man moved north and south in slow harmony with the advance and retreat of the Pleistocene ice sheets. Such movements took thousands of years to complete, so that we should not think of man as consciously retreating and advancing before the ice, but rather moving extremely slowly with other life forms. In any case, it is not until the beginning of the fourth glaciation that large numbers of men remained in frigid Europe. In one respect, he could do so at this time since he had finally developed his culture to a point where it would enable him to exist in a more severe environment. Severe perhaps, but glacial Europe was the home of vast numbers of large game animals, and staying was worth it. In any case, whether partly in response to the demands of the environment, or because man could respond positively for the first time due to the level he had reached in cultural development, it is during the fourth glaciation, 45,000 to 10,000 years ago, that man's culture, as shown by archaeological evidence, becomes rapidly more complex. Hundreds of tool types now exist where there had been relatively few. Furthermore, man appears to have become more efficient in using his raw materials. Many more tools can be made from the same amount of raw material by the techniques of the late Paleolithic than could be produced in the beginning. It has been estimated that man was getting one hundred times as much usable cutting edge from the same amount of stone at the end of the Paleolithic than he was at the beginning. This is certainly a striking statement of efficiency in terms of a ratio between what is put in and what is gotten out of any system. By the close of the Paleolithic, this efficiency had led to tool complexes of needles, scrapers, knives, engraving tools, harpoons, spearheads, and a host of other types. It is to this final phase of the Paleolithic that the brilliant cave art of Europe is dated; evidence of man's aesthetic abilities as well as the development of a systematic set of religious beliefs, since the paintings are usually thought to have some magical purpose involved with the hunt.

When the Pleistocene ended with the final retreat of the ice, the highly developed cultures of glacial Europe and elsewhere were required to shift their emphasis in terms of the way man made a living. The Paleolithic is defined as that period when man the hunter worked out an adaptation to the problems of Pleistocene existence. Now all had changed, and the following stage, known as the Mesolithic, represents and is defined as the period of man's adaptation to the modern, post-glacial environment. The Mesolithic, and those stages which follow it, have no sharp temporal limits. There are people yet today who live in a way very similar to that of the early Mesolithic inhabitants of the Old World. Developmental stages, with the exception of the Paleolithic which is partly defined in terms of a time-bounded event—the Pleistocene—do not have inherent time limits, and at most times since the end of the Pleistocene, different stages have been contemporary, depending on the part of the world under consideration. Thus while the Mesolithic ends in the Near East as early as 8000 B.C., it is still a going concern in Northern Europe 4000 years or more later. Mesolithic cultures of the Old World are characterized by a somewhat closer "keying in" to specific environmental situations. While Paleolithic cultures seem quite alike over large areas of space and through long periods of time during the Mesolithic, there is considerable variation from place to place. The preservation and completeness of the archaeological record doubtless tend to emphasize this impression but even allowing for such factors, the difference seems genuinely real. In Europe for example, there was a large number of separate Mesolithic cultures, some adapted to grassland hunting, some to life in the deep forest, and still others to shellfish collecting on the coast or the highly efficient exploitation of a number of marine resources combined with terrestrial hunting. In fact, the first extensive utilization of molluscan foods on inland waterways and marine beaches dates to this stage. There are other Mesolithic innovations, including the domestication of the dog by man, or vice versa, and the bow and arrow. In Northern Europe, it appears that Mesolithic man even discovered the art of pottery manufacture independently of the same invention far to the south in the Near East.

One important factor in the closer environmental adaptation which appears to be characteristic of the Mesolithic is the stability of the population. Whereas during the Paleolithic there seems to have been considerable mobility of individual communities, this slows down during the Mesolithic, and in one sense, preconditions man for the following Neolithic stage. Somewhat more fixed populations insure a somewhat more rapid diffusion of ideas between groups, since regular networks of cultural exchange can come into being, and given this situation, any invention which is made in one place would spread to other locations somewhat more rapidly. The development of such diffusion spheres probably made the introduction of farming during the Neolithic more efficient.

The Mesolithic stage is followed by the Neolithic in the Old World. Until recently, the Neolithic stage was identified primarily by the appearance of polished stone tools and pottery—narrow criteria which are now seen as secondary to the most important aspect of Neolithic cultures, the production of food. Man's control of his food supply through the domestication of plants and animals must rank as one of the most important events in human prehistory. Until the Neolithic, man existed by foraging and hunting, a way of life which seldom held an absolute guarantee of ample food. With the ability to produce and store as surplus the products of cultivation and animal husbandry, a more settled life resulted. Since man was not as much a pawn of his environment when he could produce a food surplus, and since not as much effort was needed to obtain the same amount of food, more experimentation was possible and the rate of cultural innovation and development increased. Not only was more spare time available, but it could be scheduled in a more efficient manner. Because of this dramatic change in his way of life, man settled in ever larger communities during the Neolithic and added new dimensions to his culture. In fact, until settled life of the type made possible by the Neolithic had come into existence, further development of culture, ultimately to civilization, could not have taken place.

Archaeologists distinguish two separate centers in which the initial change from hunting to food production occurred in the Old World, one in southwestern Asia, and one in southeastern Asia. These developments seem totally separate, although the far eastern one is a later event than its near eastern counterpart. In southwestern Asia, the Neolithic stage began sometime between 7000 and 8000 B.C. on the basis of present evidence. While this was the area of origin, it was not long until Neolithic patterns of life diffused into Europe and Africa. Egypt was drawn into the sphere quite early, before 5000 B.C., and there are Neolithic sites in southeastern Europe which date to 6000 B.C. The Neolithic economy spread rapidly into Europe along a number of routes. In some areas, this diffusion is secondary; in others, such as the coast and islands of the Mediterranean, true population movements seem to have occurred. By 3500 B.C., Neolithic cultures had replaced their Mesolithic antecedents over almost all of Europe, and influence from the Near East had reached as far east as northern China by 2000 B.C. While some of these cultures were based primarily on a combination of plant and animal domestication, certain Neolithic cultures of the Asiatic grasslands seem to have been the product of a distinctive pattern of pastoralism, using cattle, and later horses, as the primary herd animals. Steppe herders of this type are present even today in parts of Central Asia—Neolithic peoples in many ways who have survived into the present.

The southeastern Neolithic is imperfectly known; preservation is poor in the tropical areas of southeastern Asia, and far less archaeological research has been carried out there. Yet there is sufficient evidence to infer a truly separate origin for this pattern. Crops in southeastern Asia—rice, sweet potatoes, and other root crops, as well as chickens and pigs— contrast sharply with the wheat, barley and rye, and cattle, horses, sheep, and goats of the southwestern Neolithic. Although the origins of the Southeast Asiatic Neolithic are shrouded in the veil of the past, its influence is clearly visible; all the cultures of Oceania and Indonesia which cultivate are derivatives of this original culture. China seems to have fallen into both spheres of Neolithic influence, with the northern area receiving influence from the west, and southern China more closely linked with the eastern center. We are not even certain of the date of the eastern Neolithic, although slim evidence indicates it is probably prior to 2500 B.C. and perhaps considerably earlier.

The truly revolutionary events and inventions of the Neolithic set the stage for the next major development in the Old World, the rise of civilization in those areas where Neolithic cultures first appeared. Early civilizations in the Old World are placed in a developmental stage known as the Bronze Age. The term for this stage again indicates the narrow criteria used earlier as primary indicators. Bronze technology certainly appears at this time, but the Bronze Age of the Near East is far more than a series of cultures who knew how to alloy copper and tin. In Mesopotamia, civilization is attained by 3500 B.C. By civilization we mean a level of complexity marked by the presence of most of a set of criteria which includes literacy; a strong, probably theocratic central political structure which transcends the level of the individual community; monumental, highly specialized architecture such as temples and pyramids; a strong development in the arts; and true cities. All these things develop out of the Neolithic base in the Near East between 8000 and 3500 B.C., and with the appearance of the early Bronze Age civilizations of this area, we move from prehistory to history, since the early Sumerians of Mesopotamia were literate and recorded their history in a form which can be read today. The Aegean area of southeastern Europe followed close behind, with Bronze Age cultures developing there by 3000 B.C., leading ultimately to the brilliant climaxes of Mycenaean Greece and Minoan Crete. Egypt developed a true civilization at almost the same time, and in this case, bronze technology is one criterion which is relatively rare until much later. To the east, a unique civilization appears during the third millennium B.C. in the Indus Valley of Pakistan. With no written records on which to proceed, our knowledge of the Indus civilization is based entirely on archaeological study. This has revealed a culture with large cities, with remarkably modern sewage and plumbing facilities, a strikingly conservative pattern of change through time which suggests almost dictatorial central control.

If Dynastic Egypt is of the Bronze Age stage of development, yet has little bronze technology, the European continent shows just the opposite pattern. In Europe, those cultures placed in the Bronze Age are not civilizations, but they do possess the knowledge of bronze manufacture. This seeming paradox serves to highlight the somewhat arbitrary nature of developmental stages. The Bronze Age of Europe, which lasts from about 2000 B.C. until about 700 B.C. is characterized by a series of cultures which were probably not too different from the earlier cultures of the Neolithic in terms of political and social organization. There is no brilliant development in Europe like that of Sumerian Mesopotamia, and most of Europe was not brought into the realm of civilization until after the time of the Romans. However, the criterion of bronze technology, which looms large in the European case, does suggest a basic difference between the European Bronze Age and the preceding Neolithic. Bronze is an alloy, and it is a rare occasion to find areas where copper and tin ores occur together. So to alloy bronze and make tools from it, trade between areas becomes vitally necessary. There were some areas of Europe, particularly the northern area, which had spectacular Bronze Age developments, but lacked both ores, and relied on trade to obtain all their bronze. This is not to suggest that trade did not play an important part in some Neolithic cultures of Europe, but that it became more important, and in some ways, a *sine qua non* of the Bronze Age of Europe. It is during this time that the peoples of Europe become intimately related to the civilizations to the south and east. One of the most important dimensions of Bronze Age developments in Europe was the trade of amber from peoples around the Baltic Sea for bronze in finished and raw form from the south. The route of this trade, known as the Amber Route, became the focus of much of the cultural development of Central Europe at this time. There was probably a large amount of personal contact between far distant areas as well; it was discovered recently that the stones of Stonehenge bear carvings of a Mycenaean dagger and a Minoan double-bitted axe, both typical of the Aegean area.

In China, a Bronze Age civilization developed in the Yellow river valley around 1500 B.C., on the earlier Neolithic base. This was a brilliant development, and is represented by the first two recorded dynasties of Chinese history, the Shang and Chou. These people were responsible for making some of the finest bronze art objects the world has ever known, and

Shang and Chou bronzes are eagerly sought after by art museums and collectors today.

The fifth and final developmental stage in Old World prehistory is the Iron Age; like the earlier Bronze Age, it is identified in terms of a change in technology. The Iron Age of the Near East is within the range of recorded history; its influence in Europe is seen archaeologically in a true prehistoric sense. The introduction of iron into continental Europe was brought about by Greek colonists in Italy and southern France. The Bronze Age of Greece was terminated by the Dorian Invasion in 1150 B.C., plunging Greece into a period in which written history lapsed and introducing iron technology at the same time. By 700 B.C. the Greek colonies in Italy and France were diffusing iron tools and technological knowledge north into the transalpine area. Iron Age cultures of continental Europe are essentially Bronze Age cultures with iron technology added; that is, no profound transformation occurs. The subsequent development in Europe into later Iron Age cultures ultimately leads to such historically known peoples as the Gauls, the Germans, and the Celts. Certain other important innovations spread through the European and Mediterranean area during the Iron Age. Chief among these were the very important introductions of the true alphabet by the Phoenicians, and coinage by the Lydians. Both of these inventions were significant to the development of trade and commerce in the late prehistoric world of Europe and western Asia.

Iron Age culture appears in China at about the time of the turn of the Christian era with the Han Dynasty (206 B.C. to A.D. 220). It is during the Han Dynasty that Iron Age influences reach Japan, and even diffuse as far north as the American Arctic, where iron artifacts have been identified as ultimately derivative from Asia.

The prehistory of the Americas parallels that of the Old World in a striking fashion. There is little question that these developments were separate phenomena, and as such each serves as a unique comparative example for the other. That these developments show a number of striking parallels suggests that there are certain general patterns of cultural development which are in the nature of universals. Anthropologists are aware of this parallelism, and are using comparative data from Old and New World prehistory to attempt to state general "laws" of cultural development, which might ultimately lead to statements similar to those governing organic evolution, which are stated in terms of such universal forces as mutation and selection as determinants of development.[26]

The five stages of New World prehistory—the Lithic, Archaic, Formative, Classic, and Post-Classic—have certain similarities to the five Old World stages.[27] It is significant that the New World terms apply to stages more similar to those of the Old World than the differences in the terms for them might suggest. The reason for this difference is that such terms as Paleolithic or Bronze Age were coined in the early days of archaeology, and reflect a stress on certain criteria which are not seen as important today. The New World stage designations indicate process in a more general sense than do their Old World equivalents.

The Lithic stage is the New World Paleolithic, and represents that period when the first men crossed into North America via the Bering Strait. It is believed today that this crossing took place some 20,000 years ago, during the last glaciation. Evidence of these first Americans is in the form of stone tools and, less frequently, tools of bone, associated with the remains of such extinct animal forms as the mammoth and a large species of bison. The earliest sites representing these hunters are found over much of North America, and there are a few to the south in Mexico and South America, although these latter occurrences are not nearly as numerous or as reliable as the North American material. As time passed, the distribution of sites representing early man in North America became more restricted to the Great Plains grasslands; perhaps the last large herds of large bison and mammoth were limited to this region as the forest returned in the wake of the retreating ice. Many of these sites are kill sites, marking places where

[26] J. Steward, "Cultural Causality and Law: A Trial Formulation," *Theory of Culture Change* (Urbana: University of Illinois Press, 1955).

[27] New World Stage Definitions are from G. R. Willey and P. Phillips, *Method and Theory in American Archeology* (Chicago: University of Chicago Press, Phoenix Books, 1962).

game was killed and butchered, rather than living areas. Man had reached the extreme southern tip of the South American continent by at least 7000 B.C., as shown by a pair of caves in the Fuegian area with Lithic stage components at the base of their deposits, and a radiocarbon date indicating the age.

Much as the Mesolithic stage of Europe reflects man's adjustment to the changes of the post-glacial world, so the Archaic is identified in the New World by similar criteria. We should not think of man's initial entry into the New World as having been a single episode. Other people followed over the years, and many of the changes seen in the Archaic probably represent innovations which occurred in Asia or even Europe. Bows and arrows make their appearance during the Archaic, as does the domesticated dog. The closer adaptation to discrete environmental niches is seen also in the New World, and shellfish collecting as a major subsistence technique makes its appearance.

The Archaic is followed by the Formative stage, analogous to the Neolithic, and identified by the domestication of plants and, to a much lesser extent than in the Old World, of animals. Man didn't have such suitable wild animals to start with in the Americas, and after thousands of years, the first Europeans to arrive found the Indians with a rather thin inventory of domesticated animals—turkeys, llamas and their relatives, dogs, guinea pigs, and Muscovy ducks almost exhaust the list. The absence of an efficient animal for traction, such as the horse or ox, may well have influenced the course of cultural development in a rather profound manner. It is striking that the wheel, a mainstay of Old World culture since the Neolithic, was never invented in the New World as a utilitarian device. That the Americans knew about the principle of the wheel is shown by small, wheeled toy dogs found at several Mexican sites. Yet it apparently was never put to work to man's benefit, and this curious absence might in some way relate to the lack of a suitable draft animal to supply traction.

The plant foods of the American Formative include maize, beans, squash, potatoes, and manioc. There is no question that this complex of cultivated plants is truly separate from any of the Old World. While there is evidence of incipient domestication of these plant foods several thousand years before Christ, a fully developed Formative level of culture, with all the benefits which derive from a productive economy, does not seem to have appeared much before 1500 B.C. The earliest locations of Formative culture are the Valley of Mexico, parts of Guatemala, and the Peruvian area. These areas within Nuclear America were to be the scene of the first flowering of American civilization at a later time, much as early Old World civilizations first appeared in the same area where the Neolithic had its early beginnings.

The Formative way of life spread slowly into many parts of the American continents, and by the time of the European conquest, all tropical America, as well as North America except for the Pacific coast, plateau and basin areas, and arctic and subarctic regions had acquired the knowledge of food production. Formative cultures begin in North America as early as a century or two before Christ, and reach local elaborations or climaxes in the American Southwest and Southeast. In the Southwest, the well-known pueblo cultures are typical of the Formative cultures of the area, and in the Southeast large villages with earthen pyramids surmounted by thatched roof wattle and daub temples are faint echoes of the more civilized cultures of Mexico to the south. North America was also the location of a rich Formative development which occurred without benefit of farming or animal domestication. This unique pattern was typical of the Northwest Coast area of Alaska and British Columbia, where the Indians were so favored by bountiful natural resources, including salmon and game, that they were able to attain great heights of artistic, political, and social achievement in the absence of a productive economy.

The Classic stage of New World culture history is the time of civilization. The criteria which we saw as characteristic of Old World civilization apply also in the New, with monumental architecture, brilliant artistic achievements, mathematics, strong theocratic government, and literacy of a kind all occurring. The beginnings of the Classic stage fall in the general vicinity of the turn of the Christian era, and civilization developed in the entire area from central Mexico south to Guatemala, Honduras, and El Salvador, and again in the Peruvian Andes. The early civilizations in these areas were

all somewhat different, and each was distinctive for some particular achievement. Among the Maya, astronomy, mathematics, and the calendar were all highly developed. The
Maya invented the concept of zero and place value before it
was invented in the Old World, and the Maya calendar was
more accurate than the one we use today. The early
Mexicans created the first true urban complex in the New
World, which can be seen today at the immense site of Teotihuacán near Mexico City. In the Peruvian area, elaboration
of the arts of metallurgy, textiles, and ceramics was especially
high.

The Post-Classic stage brings us to the end of indigenous
cultural development in the New World, and it was Post-
Classic civilizations which the Spanish encountered and con-
quered in the Aztec and Inca. The Post-Classic, which begins
between about A.D. 700 and 1000 in different parts of civilized
America, is identified on the basis of a trend to secularization
in political organization with the decline of the theocracy of
Classic times, an increased emphasis on militarism, and colonial expansion, particularly marked among the Aztec and
Inca, and something of a decline in the vigor, but not technical quality, of various arts, including architecture and ceramics. Urban concentrations of the type typical of the Mexican
Classic became widespread during the Post-Classic of both
Central and South America.

The development of New World culture was cut short by
the arrival of the European colonial powers between the fif-
teenth and eighteenth centuries, but prior to the period of
European conquest, the Americans had indeed shown a
development of culture from humble Lithic origins which is
remarkably similar to that of the Old World, even though
we are virtually certain that there was little or no contact
throughout the time in question.

This thumbnail sketch of world culture history serves at
least to clarify the concept of the developmental stage. We
have said that stages, although arbitrary, are in one way
manifestations of the behavioral aspect of patterning seen in
whole societies. This is certainly true, since though the stage
might be arbitrarily delineated, it does permit the grouping
of numbers of prehistoric cultures in broad behavioral cate-

gories—similarities in subsistence, settlement size, artistic achievement or material assemblages dictate the assignment of cultures to different stages, and these similarities are ultimately a function of similarities in the behavior which produced them. We have seen that beyond the developmental stage, as it applies to a single hemisphere, there are broader similarities which are truly worldwide. The theocratic bias of early civilizations, whether in Mesopotamia or Peru, the pattern of ecological adaptation following the Pleistocene, and the invention or adoption of food production are but a few of the worldwide similarities exhibited by most cultures as they develop through time. We might therefore suggest yet a sixth level of behavior, which in the manner in which it represents patterning universal to the entire human species, might be seen as something approaching what many people call "human nature."

It is a long way between laying out a five-foot-square pit on a site and speculating about similarities between groups of men on a worldwide scale, yet such speculation would be completely idle, and potentially sterile, unless countless five-foot pits had been laid out and excavated in the past. Archaeology embraces the entire spectrum between these extremes, and tells us much about man's past. From the regularities which we can see in this past existence, combined with the patterning which anthropologists delineate from observing people living today, we stand to gain a more perfect understanding of ourselves, a most vital and desirable goal in the complex and troubled world of today.

Chapter IX

ARCHAEOLOGY TOMORROW

Archaeology is truly an infant discipline. Its parent, anthropology, is scarcely a century old; as the child, it is even younger. Stratigraphic excavation was not done systematically until the early years of the twentieth century; carbon-14 dating is but eighteen years old, and the corpus of anthropological theory upon which sound archaeology must rest has only become truly useful during the past thirty years. Compared with such venerable disciplines as physics, chemistry, and biology, archaeology can claim no long development, and few thoroughly tried and true methods and theories.

It is therefore not surprising that in many ways "scientific" archaeology is just now barely coming of age. Exciting developments in archaeological method and theory have been increasing rapidly in the past decade; most of the approaches and methods outlined in this book are scarcely twenty years old, and nearly all belong to this century.

What can we expect in the years to come? For archaeologists, who are concerned with the past, predictions seem perilous and uncertain, yet there are certain trends apparent within archaeology today which indicate the developments of tomorrow. One of the most exciting and potentially productive areas of archaeology in the sixties is the application of that wonder of the mid-twentieth century, the computer. The first use of computers in archaeology was in 1960; today there are numerous studies, some already in published form, and many others in process, which depend on the use of high-speed computation equipment for their ultimate success. Since archaeological data are so diverse and numerous, the use of computers becomes essential to discern patterning in these data, to derive statistical expressions of the significance and reliability of these patterns, and to manipulate massive quantities of data, such as the attributes of a collection of 20,000 stone tools. Computers can even produce printed maps of the spatial and temporal distributions of any measurable archaeological information, adding an exciting graphic dimension to their application in modern archaeology.

Archaeologists are becoming increasingly aware of the urgency of articulating their data with that of general ethnography and ethnology, and as greater effort is made to connect people and objects in a systematic manner, more imaginative but at the same time more sound inferences will result. It is in this direction that portions of this book are directed; we can expect broader applications of such a perspective in the years to come.

It is both significant and noteworthy that the trends which characterize archaeological development today are in those aspects which pertain to analysis of the data following excavation. Excavation, integration, and inference, the three levels of archaeological research, have developed in that order. Excavation and its techniques were the first to receive attention and refinement; this was followed by a period when various integrative methods were devised, and only recently have the inferential aspects of archaeology been the object of the attention and development devoted to the other elements of the discipline. Since the ultimate end of all archaeology is the fleshing out in cultural terms of the basic data, we can confidently expect new and sophisticated emphasis on the aspects of inference to produce exciting results in the very near future. It is through such inference, done with imagination and insight, that archaeology takes its proper place within the field of anthropology and the social sciences. If it does not occupy such a status at this moment, we can be confident that it will in the very near future.

APPENDIX
A typical type description

PASTE

Tempering Grit, diameters ranging from −0.5 to 2.0 mm. The appearance and composition (quartz, mica, and a little feldspar) suggest that the tempering material is a decomposed granite.

Texture Medium to coarse.

Hardness 3.0–4.0.

Color Tan to dark gray; exterior surfaces often heavily carboned.

FORM

Overall shape Jars with collared rims, constricted necks, rounded shoulders, and rounded bottoms.

Lip Rounded, occasionally thickened by the addition of a small bracing fillet on the exterior surface.

Rim All the rims are collared. The collars range from 24 to 55 mm. in height. Interior and exterior profiles are more or less parallel to each other, forming a straight or concave plane which extends downward and outward from the lip. The lower edge of the collar is marked by a fairly abrupt shoulder which forms the junction between the collar and the low curved neck. The bottom of the collar is sometimes scalloped. Below the neck, the vessel wall turns outward toward the shoulder. These rims might be contrasted with the rims of the Foreman types by describing them as Z-rims rather than S-rims, since the surface is flat or concave rather than convex.

Neck A relatively low, constricted zone below the shoulder of the rim.

FROM: D. J. Lehmer, *Archaeological Investigations in the Oahe Dam Area, South Dakota, 1950–51,* Bureau of American Ethnology, Bulletin 158, 1954.

Shoulder Rounded.

Base Rounded.

HANDLES One sherd has a short tablike lug extending down from the lower edge of the collar in the same plane as the face of the collar itself. Two others have fractured areas which seem to indicate the presence of loop handles running from the base of the rim collar to the shoulder of the vessel.

SURFACE FINISH Bodies simple stamped, some with extensive plain areas. The stamping on one of the restored vessels is vertical. Necks are plain or brushed vertically; interior surfaces are plain.

DECORATION The decoration is confined to the rim and lip. It is preponderantly cord impressed. Patterns consist of a series of horizontal lines, or a series of interlocking triangles filled alternately with horizontal and diagonal cord impressions. The cord-impressed zone is sometimes bordered by a series of punctations. Two pieces were decorated with diagonal broad-trailed lines, and one was plain except for a series of punctations at the base of the rim.

REMARKS A number of the pieces assigned to Colombe Collared Rim at the Phillips Ranch site show a considerable similarity to some Lower Loup sherds from Nebraska. The most striking difference is in the incised decoration on the Nebraska pieces and the predominantly cord-impressed decoration on the Phillips Ranch rims.

SELECTED READINGS

General

Clark, J. G. D., *Archaeology and Society; Reconstructing the Prehistoric Past* (University Paperbacks); London: Methuen, 1960.

Heizer, Robert F. (ed.), *The Archaeologist at Work; A Source Book of Archaeological Method and Interpretation.* New York: Harper and Row, 1959.

Hole, Frank, and Heizer, Robert F., *An Introduction to Prehistoric Archeology.* New York: Holt, Rinehart & Winston, 1965.

Excavation

Heizer, Robert F. (ed.), *A Guide to Archaeological Field Methods.* Millbrae, California: National Press, 1958.

Kenyon, Kathleen M., *Beginning in Archaeology.* New York: Praeger, 1961.

Wheeler, R. E. M., *Archaeology from the Earth.* Baltimore: Pelican Books, 1956.

Chronology

Ford, James A., *A Quantitative Method for Deriving Cultural Chronology.* Washington: Pan American Union, 1962.

Zeuner, Friedrich E., *Dating the Past; An Introduction to Geochronology.* London: Methuen, 1958.

Laboratory Procedures

Plenderleith, Harold J., *The Conservation of Antiquities and Works of Art; Treatment, Repair and Restoration.* London: Oxford University Press, 1956.

Shepard, Anna O., *Ceramics for the Archaeologist* (Carnegie Institute of Washington Publication, No. 609); Washington, 1956.

Site Reports

Brew, John O., *The Archaeology of Alkali Ridge, South-eastern Utah* (Papers of the Peabody Museum of Archeology and Ethnology, No. 21); Cambridge, 1946.

Clark, J. G. D., *Excavations at Star Carr; An Early Mesolithic Site at Seamer near Scarborough, Yorkshire.* London: Cambridge University Press, 1955.

Cotter, J., *Archaeological Excavations at Jamestown, Virginia.* Washington: Archaeological Research Series, National Park Service, 1958.

Di Peso, Charles C., et al., *The Upper Pima of San Cayetano del Tumacacori.* Dragoon, Arizona: Amerind Foundation Publication, No. 7, 1957.

Prehistory

Clark, J. G. D., *Prehistoric Europe: The Economic Basis.* London: Methuen, 1952.

Ehrich, Robert W. (ed.), *Relative Chronologies in Old World Archeology.* Chicago: University of Chicago Press, 1954.

Jennings, Jesse D., and Norbeck, Edward (eds.), *Prehistoric Man in the New World.* Chicago: University of Chicago Press, 1964.

Piggot, Stuart (ed.), *The Dawn of Civilization.* New York: McGraw-Hill, 1961.

Method and Theory

Rouse, I., *Prehistory in Haiti, A Study in Method* (Yale University Publications in Anthropology, No. 21); New Haven, 1939.

Taylor, Walter W., *A Study of Archeology* (American Anthropological Association Memoir, No. 69); Menasha, Wisconsin, 1948.

Willey, Gordon R., and Phillips, Philip, *Method and Theory in American Archeology.* Chicago: University of Chicago Press, 1958.

INDEX